D1523354

NAZI PROPAGANDA
JEWS IN HITLER'S GERMANY

PUBLIC PERSECUTIONS   Kate Shoup

Cavendish
Square

New York

Published in 2017 by Cavendish Square Publishing, LLC
243 5th Avenue, Suite 136, New York, NY 10016

Copyright © 2017 by Cavendish Square Publishing, LLC

First Edition

Website: cavendishsq.com

This publication represents the opinions and views of the author based on
his or her personal experience, knowledge, and research. The information
in this book serves as a general guide only. The author and publisher
have used their best efforts in preparing this book and disclaim liability
rising directly or indirectly from the use and application of this book.

CPSIA Compliance Information: Batch #CW17CSQ

All websites were available and accurate when this book was sent to press.

Library of Congress Cataloging-in-Publication Data

Names: Shoup, Kate.
Title: Nazi propaganda: Jews in Hitler's Germany / Kate Shoup.
Description: New York : Cavendish Square, 2017. |
Series: Public persecutions | Includes index.
Identifiers: ISBN 9781502623218 (library bound) | ISBN 9781502623225 (ebook)
Subjects: LCSH: Holocaust, Jewish (1939-1945)–Juvenile literature.
| Jews–Persecutions–Germany–Juvenile literature. | World War,
1939-1945–Jews–Juvenile literature. | Germany–History–1933-1945–
Juvenile literature. | Germany–Ethnic relations–Juvenile literature.
Classification: LCC D804.34 S47 2017 | DD 940.53' 18 –dc23

Editorial Director: David McNamara
Editor: Fletcher Doyle
Copy Editor: Nathan Heidelberger
Associate Art Director: Amy Greenan
Designer: Stephanie Flecha
Production Coordinator: Karol Szymczuk

The photographs in this book are used by permission and through the courtesy of:
Cover, 12, 75 Universal History Archive/Universal Images Group/Getty Images; pp. 4, 56, 78, 104 Bettmann/
Getty Images; p. 7 New York Times Co./Archive Photos/Getty Images; p. 8 Three Lions/Hulton Archive/Getty
Images; p. 15 Everett Historical/Shutterstock.com; p. 22 Johannes Simon/Getty Images; p. 25 File:Riksdagsbrannen.
jpg/Wikimedia Commons; pp. 28, 50, 62, 63, 94 ullstein bild/Getty Images; p. 30 Print Collector/Hulton
Archive/Getty Images; pp. 35, 38, 65 Universal Images Group/Getty Images; pp. 45, 110 © AP Images; p.
47 Imagno/Hulton Archive/Getty Images; pp. 76, 86, 90 Sovfoto/Universal Images Group/Getty Images; p.
82 AFP/Getty Images; p. 96 Central Press/Hulton Archive/Getty Images; p. 101 Horace Abrahams/Hulton
Archive/Getty Images; p. 108 NASRA/File:Nuremberg trials 281431M original.jpg/Wikimedia Commons.

Printed in the United States of America

Contents

Time of Destruction

Between 1939 and 1945, the German government, led by Adolf Hitler and the Nazi Party, methodically slaughtered some 6 million European Jews—about two-thirds of all Jews in Europe. Of these, 1.5 million were children. Today, we call this murderous campaign the **Holocaust**. The Holocaust is also known as the Shoah, which is Hebrew for "destruction."

The Holocaust coincided with World War II. This war pitted the Axis Powers (Germany, Italy, and Japan) against the Allied Powers (Great Britain, France, the Soviet Union, the United States, and China). It started in 1939, with the German invasion of Poland. In 1940 and 1941, Germany conquered Denmark, Norway, Belgium, the Netherlands, Luxembourg, France, Yugoslavia, and Greece. With each victory, the Nazis gained territory—and with it, access to yet more Jews. Allied forces finally defeated the Nazis in May 1945.

Opposite: Surviving prisoners who were used as slave labor at the Ebensee concentration camp, in Austria, were liberated on May 9, 1945.

The Holocaust was an act of **genocide**. According to the United Nations Convention on the Prevention and Punishment of the Crime of Genocide, genocide describes "any of the following acts committed with intent to destroy, in whole or in part, a national, ethnical, racial, or religious group." The acts in question include "killing members of the group," "causing serious bodily or mental harm to members of the group," "deliberately inflicting on the group conditions of life calculated to bring about its physical destruction in whole or in part," "imposing measures intended to prevent births within the group," and "forcibly transferring children of the group to another group."

How did the Nazis murder so many Jews? They developed quick and efficient killing methods that enabled them to slaughter Jews in an assembly-line manner. In some killing facilities, Nazis massacred as many as eight thousand Jews each day. Why did ordinary German citizens (and later, citizens of the territories that Germany conquered) allow these killings to happen? This question is more difficult to answer. One reason is that the Nazis engaged in a systematic effort to dehumanize the Jews. To achieve this, they blamed the Jews for Germany's defeat in World War I and for its dismal situation in the aftermath, they passed anti-Jewish laws, and they spread anti-Jewish **propaganda**. As a result, many ordinary citizens simply did not view Jews as human beings. Another reason is that many ordinary citizens benefited from the absence of the Jews. These citizens took their jobs and acquired their property. A third reason is that the Nazis severely punished anyone who attempted to help the Jews.

Children were indoctrinated early by the Nazis. Here, a group from the Hitler Youth marches in front of saluting adults.

This instilled fear in the general public. Finally, the Nazis conducted much of this killing in secret. Few people knew the extent of the Nazi death machine.

The Nazis sought to exterminate all Jews—an act they called the "Final Solution"—and they very nearly succeeded. Despite their efforts, thousands of Jews survived Nazi oppression to bear witness to the crimes committed against them. It is imperative that all people learn from their experience to ensure such crimes never occur again.

ONE

The Seeds of the Holocaust

When confronted with the topic of the Holocaust, people inevitably ask one question: Why? Why did the Germans hate the Jews? Why did they seek to annihilate them? There are, of course, no easy answers to these questions. After all, how could anyone explain such insanity? Still, the attempted extermination of the Jews didn't just happen. Certain events and attitudes contributed to their demise.

The seeds of the Holocaust were planted in the aftermath of World War I, then known as the Great War. This conflict commenced during the summer of 1914.

It started with the assassination of Archduke Franz Ferdinand of Austria-Hungary and his wife, Sophie, Duchess of Hohenberg, in the Bosnian city of Sarajevo. This event triggered a crisis, putting into play a series of long-established international alliances. One alliance, dubbed the Allies, consisted of the British Empire, the Russian Empire, and

Opposite: Following Germany's defeat in World War I, ordinary Germans fell into extreme poverty. Here, German women sift through garbage looking for food.

France. This alliance would ultimately expand to include Italy, Japan, and the United States. Germany and Austria-Hungary—and later, the Ottoman Empire and Bulgaria—comprised the opposing alliance, called the Central Powers.

Convinced that Serbia was behind the assassination of the archduke, the Austro-Hungarians invaded that country on July 28, 1914. The Russian Empire, under the rule of Czar Nicholas II, quickly mobilized in Serbia's defense. Around the same time, Germany—which had achieved nationhood in 1871 and was now under the rule of Kaiser Wilhelm II—successfully invaded Belgium and Luxembourg before turning its attention toward France. In response, the British Empire declared war on Germany.

The war quickly took on two fronts. On the western front, in France, the French and the British struggled to fend off the Germans. This quickly became a stalemate. Both sides suffered terrible losses, but neither gained significant ground. On the eastern front, the Russian army handily defeated the Austro-Hungarians but were soon halted by the Germans in East Prussia.

Although all parties had anticipated a quick resolution to the conflict, the war dragged on with no end in sight. That changed in March 1917, with the collapse of the Russian Empire. The Russian people, frustrated by government corruption, food shortages, and the lingering effects of a deadly and costly war, ousted Czar Nicholas II and installed a new democratic government. Six months later, leftist revolutionaries, called Bolsheviks, overthrew this new government and formed a Communist state, later called the

Union of Soviet Socialist Republics, also called the USSR or the Soviet Union. In March 1918, the Bolshevik government signed the **Treaty** of Brest-Litovsk, making peace with the Central Powers and ending its involvement in the war.

Russia's withdrawal gave the Germans an enormous advantage. Emboldened, they redoubled their efforts on the western front in the spring of 1918. But the Allies, which now included the United States, beat them back. At the same time, the British navy blockaded German ports, stemming the flow of supplies for the German war effort and food for the German populace. Soon, it became clear that Germany would lose the war. On November 11, Germany signed an **armistice** with the Allies, conceding defeat and ending a war that had claimed millions of lives.

The Paris Peace Conference and the Treaty of Versailles

In 1919, the Allies convened in Paris for the Paris Peace Conference. There, they discussed the terms of the armistice (albeit without the input of the Central Powers) and composed the treaties that would officially end the Great War.

Before the end of the war, US president Woodrow Wilson delivered a speech called the "Fourteen Points." It offered a roadmap to world peace. Among other things, this speech called for an end to secret treaties, a reduction of arms, reduced colonial claims, freedom of the seas, and the removal of economic barriers between countries. It also proposed the formation of a League of Nations, a global organization that would, in Wilson's words, ensure the "political independence and territorial integrity [of] great and small states alike." The Central Powers—and Wilson—believed that these Fourteen Points would serve as the foundation of the peace agreement.

They were wrong. Britain, France, and Italy seemed more interested in punishing the Central Powers—especially Germany—than in forging a lasting peace. To that end, their treaty with Germany demanded that "Germany [accept] the responsibility of Germany and her allies for causing all the loss and damage" during the war. It also forced Germany to disarm, permanently cut the size of its military, and surrender about a tenth of its territory. Finally, it ordered Germany to

David Lloyd George of Great Britain, Vittorio Emanuele Orlando of Italy, Georges Clemenceau of France, and Woodrow Wilson of the United States take a break from negotiations at the signing of the Treaty of Versailles.

pay **reparations**. These were later set at 132 billion gold marks, or $442 billion today. Of Wilson's Fourteen Points, only one remained: the formation of a League of Nations.

By this time, Germany had dissolved into chaos. After Germany's war defeat, Kaiser Wilhelm II **abdicated** at the urging of his top military leaders. The Germans formed a democratic government, but German revolutionaries—inspired by events in Russia—stirred up unrest. Meanwhile, the country's economy was in shambles. Given its situation, Germany had no choice but to agree to the terms of the treaty, in spite of its one-sided nature. In June 1919, Germany signed the treaty at Versailles, near Paris—hence its name, the Treaty of Versailles.

The Weimar Republic

Germany's new democratic government formed in January 1919. Due to unrest in the country's capital city, Berlin, the National Assembly could not convene there. Instead, it met in a town called Weimar. From then on, the German government—which included representatives from various walks of life, including Jews—was referred to as the Weimar Republic.

The constitution of this new government called for a president rather than a monarch. A parliament, called the Reichstag, held the president's power in check. In turn, the president held the Reichstag's power in check by appointing the chairman of that body, called the chancellor.

Several political parties shared in the governance of the Weimar Republic. This quickly became problematic, however. No one party managed to secure enough power to govern effectively. But the Weimar Republic had another problem: A significant portion of the German public blamed the politicians in this new government—most notably the Jews and Marxists—for losing the Great War. They believed German generals who claimed they would have won the war had they not been "stabbed in the back" by these disloyal officials. This belief contributed to the government's ongoing instability—and ultimately, to the advent of the Holocaust in the years to come.

The Economic Effects of the Treaty of Versailles

Germany's economic situation did little to alleviate this unrest. Before the start of the Great War, in 1914, Germany was the most economically advanced nation in Europe. But by the end of this conflict, in 1918, its economy had completely collapsed. Compounding this problem were the terms of the Treaty of Versailles, which dictated that Germany pay enormous reparations.

In late 1922, Germany defaulted on these reparations. In retaliation, French and Belgian troops invaded and occupied an industrial area of Germany called the Ruhr, in 1923. The Ruhr region was home to several German factories and coal mines, which the French and Belgians seized to offset Germany's unpaid debt. In response, the Germans who worked in these factories and mines went on strike.

The strike was effective in that it frustrated the French and the Belgians. But it did nothing to help the German

The Nazis created this poster in 1928 to show how they would deal with the Jews. Notice the stereotyped image of the victim.

economy. In fact, it contributed to a rise in **inflation**. Then, to pay its debts, the German government printed more money. This resulted in higher inflation, or hyperinflation. Before the war, 1 US dollar was equivalent to 4 German marks. By 1923, 1 US dollar equaled 4.2 trillion marks. In other words, the mark was reduced to one-trillionth of its value. During this period, a German citizen could cash in his entire life savings—and it wouldn't be enough to buy a single loaf of bread.

Finally, in 1925, American banks offered the German government a lifeline in the form of ongoing loans. Germany used these loans to pay reparations to other European nations. The same year, Germany signed the Treaty of Locarno. This treaty affirmed that Germany, France, and Belgium would respect each other's borders. Slowly, Germany's relations with other nations improved. Germany even joined the League of Nations, improving its ability to engage in international trade. Things were looking up!

This period would not last for long. In the autumn of 1929, the American stock market crashed. American banks, desperate to stem their losses, called in the loans they had made to Germany. Germany could not pay. Worse, as America plunged into the Great Depression, there was less demand for German goods. Due to these factors, plus the fact that Germany's economy was already quite fragile, Germany, too, plunged into an economic depression. Germans faced high unemployment and severe poverty. Those lucky enough to find work suffered from low wages and poor working conditions. Even the rich were not immune. As German banks failed, the wealthy lost their savings.

The German population was demoralized. Germany had lost the war. The economy was in ruins. Who was to blame? And who could save them from this nightmare? One political party, the Nazi Party, answered these questions. According to the Nazis, capitalism, the ruling class, liberalism, Communists, and trade unions were at fault. Behind all these, they claimed, were the Jews. As for the second question—who could save the Germans from this nightmare?—the Nazis put forth one man: Adolf Hitler.

Who Was Adolf Hitler?

Adolf Hitler was born to Alois and Klara Hitler on April 20, 1889. They lived in a small Austro-Hungarian town called Braunau, near the German border. Two more children, Edmund and Paula, soon followed. (Edmund would die of measles at age five.) During Hitler's early childhood, the family moved from town to town. Finally, in 1897, they settled in Leonding, where they remained for the duration of Hitler's youth.

Hitler dreamed of being an artist. His father, a customs official, wanted Hitler to follow in his footsteps. To that end, he sent Hitler to a nearby technical school instead of to art school. Hitler rebelled. He purposely earned poor grades at school. As he later wrote in his famous book, *Mein Kampf (My Struggle)*, he believed that when his father realized "what little progress I was making at the technical school he would let me devote myself to my dream." However, Hitler's father—as strong minded as his young son—did not relent. Hitler and his father remained locked in conflict until his father's sudden death in 1903.

Moved by her son's plight, Hitler's widowed mother allowed him to switch schools. In 1905, he passed his exams. Soon, he moved to Vienna to pursue a career in the arts. For a second time, Hitler's dream was denied. Twice, the Academy of Fine Arts Vienna rejected his application—first in 1907 and again in 1908—due to an "unfitness for painting." Worse, in December 1907, his mother—who had been helping to fund his adventures in Vienna—died of cancer at the age of forty-seven. With no one to support him, Hitler quickly ran out of money and lived in poverty.

In 1913, Hitler received a windfall from his father's estate. He moved to Munich, in the southern part of the German Empire known as Bavaria. A year later, the Great War broke out. Hitler joined an infantry unit in the Bavarian Reserve, on the western front. For much of the war, he was stationed at regimental headquarters, far from the fighting. However, he was present for the First Battle of Ypres, the Battle of the Somme, the Battle of Arras, and the Battle of Passchendaele. At the Somme, a shell explosion injured Hitler's left thigh. And at Passchendaele, a mustard gas attack temporarily blinded him. Still, according to the book *The Last Lion: Winston Spencer Churchill: Defender of the Realm, 1940–1965*, Hitler called Great War "the greatest of all experiences." In his mind, only the final result—Germany's defeat—was lacking. Like many Germans, particularly German soldiers, Hitler was shocked by Germany's defeat in the Great War. And like many Germans, he believed that the German army had been "stabbed in the back" by the Jews and Marxists in the new Weimar government.

After the Great War, Hitler worked as an intelligence agent for the German military. His superiors assigned him the task of infiltrating the German Worker's Party (DAP) and monitoring its activities. Hitler quickly found himself moved by the DAP's nationalist, anti-Jewish, anti-capitalist, and anti-Marxist ideals. In September 1919, at the invitation of the party's founder, Anton Drexler, Hitler joined the DAP.

Hitler's Rise to Prominence

In February 1920, Hitler delivered a speech outlining a twenty-five-point plan for the DAP, which he renamed the Nationalsozialistiche Deutsche Arbeiterpartei (National Socialist German Workers Party), or the Nazi Party. Some aspects of this plan—conceived by Drexler, Hitler, and two other party members—didn't sound so bad. It called for a system to care for the elderly and for policies to create a strong middle class. It promised a strong national education system for all. It opposed child labor. It pressed for freedom of religion. Other points were less positive. The plan demanded the "free expropriation of land," clearing the way for conquest. It called for the formation of a "strong central power" with "unlimited authority." It sought to restrict the press, noting that "Publications which are counter to the general good are to be forbidden," and called for "legal prosecution of artistic and literary forms which exert a destructive influence on our national life." Perhaps most notably, it denied Jews the right to German citizenship. "No Jew," the plan said, "may be a member of the Nation." By extension, Jews were deprived of the right live in Germany except as a guest; to hold public office; or to work as a member of the press. Finally, the plan demanded that the Treaty of Versailles be rescinded. This would enable the German government to cease payment of reparations and to rebuild its military.

In the spring of 1920, after his discharge from the military, Hitler began working full time for the Nazi Party. He designed the now-famous Nazi flag: a red background with a white circle and black swastika. In July 1921, Hitler, who by then had developed a reputation as a brilliant and charismatic public speaker able to influence large crowds, assumed control of the party, replacing Drexler as chairman. He would rule the party—and, later, Germany—in an **autocratic** manner, requiring absolute obedience.

In November 1923, members of the Nazi Party, led by Hitler, attempted a **coup** in Munich. This coup, commonly called the Beer Hall Putsch, proved unsuccessful. Bavarian officials arrested Hitler and his cohorts for high treason. During the trial, Hitler insisted that it was his selfless devotion to the *Volk*—the German people—that had inspired him to act. Nevertheless, the court convicted Hitler and sentenced him to five years in prison. Hitler did not serve his full sentence, however. After just one year, the Bavarian Supreme Court pardoned him.

Hitler's time in prison did not go to waste. During his incarceration, he wrote the first volume of *Mein Kampf*. This book—part autobiography, part manifesto—outlined Hitler's political beliefs. In the book, Hitler described Jews as "parasites." He blamed them for Germany's defeat in the Great War. "If at the beginning of the War and during the War twelve or fifteen thousand of these Hebrew corrupters of the people had been held under poison gas, as happened to hundreds of thousands of our very best German workers in the field, the sacrifice of millions at the front would not have been in vain," he wrote. In his view, the Jews were also at fault for the country's ensuing economic problems. He therefore called for their destruction—which, he admitted, "must necessarily be a bloody process."

Hitler believed members of the Germanic and Nordic races, the so-called **Aryans**, were a master race. To Hitler, the ideal Aryan was blond, blue-eyed, and tall (strangely, Hitler himself had dark hair and dark eyes, and was of average height). Germany, Hitler claimed in *Mein Kampf*, could prosper only under Aryan rule. To ensure "racial purity," Hitler called for the annihilation of non-Aryans, such as the Jews. Germans should, he said, "occupy themselves not merely with the breeding of dogs, horses, and cats but also with care for the purity of their own blood," noting that "all who are not of a good race are chaff." Hitler also argued in *Mein Kampf* that Germany should conquer the territory to the east, currently settled by so-called lesser people, to give the master race space to flourish—a policy known as *Lebensraum* (German for "living space"). *Mein Kampf* was very influential, inspiring much of the German populace to adopt Hitler's anti-Jewish views.

Hitler's message grew even more compelling after the US stock market crashed in 1929, plunging Germany into despair once again. Hitler's promise to renounce the terms of the Treaty of Versailles—specifically, discontinuing payments of reparations and rebuilding the military—resonated with the German people. So did Hitler's continued scapegoating of the Jews for nearly every aspect of Germany's decline, including its defeat in the Great War. In 1930, the Nazi Party became the second-largest party in office, securing 18.3 percent of the vote and 107 parliamentary seats. In 1932, the Nazis did even better. They secured 37 percent of the vote, making it the largest single party in the Reichstag.

The next year, on January 30, 1933, President Paul von Hindenburg appointed Hitler chancellor of Germany. This was in part an effort to keep Hitler under control. Franz von Papen, Hitler's vice-chancellor, boasted that "in two months, we will have pushed Hitler into a corner so that he squeaks." The vice-chancellor was mistaken. Hitler's reign was only just beginning.

Hermann Göring

Hermann Göring was one of Hitler's henchmen. Göring joined the Nazi Party in 1923 after hearing a speech by Hitler.

Göring was involved in the Beer Hall Putsch. During this attempted coup, he was shot in the leg. Göring evaded arrest and escaped to Austria for medical attention. To ease his pain, doctors gave Göring morphine. This was the start of a morphine addiction that plagued Göring until the end of his life.

As Hitler ascended to power, Göring—who had been a highly decorated fighter pilot in the Great War—enjoyed a position of privilege in his government. Indeed, for a time, Göring was designated as Hitler's successor and the deputy of all his

Copies of Hitler's book, *Mein Kampf*, in which he spelled out his plans for the Jews.

offices. He founded the fearsome Geheime Staatspolizei (Secret State Police), or the Gestapo for short. (He later surrendered command of this organization to another henchman, Heinrich Himmler.) He also served as commander in chief of the German Luftwaffe (air force).

By 1943, Göring's star had fallen within Hitler's regime. This was because of the Luftwaffe's failure to stop the bombing of German cities by Allied forces, as well as its inability to resupply German forces pinned down in Stalingrad in the USSR. Ultimately, Hitler would strip Göring of his positions and expel him from the party.

At the end of the war, Göring was convicted of war crimes and crimes against humanity and sentenced to hang. Before the sentence could be carried out, he committed suicide by ingesting a cyanide pill.

Hitler Claims Absolute Power

Hitler understood that to enact his plans to exterminate the Jews, he needed absolute power. As a first step, he enlisted members of the Nazi Party to act as auxiliary police. He endowed members of his own protective squad, called the Schutzstaffel, or SS, with police power. Members of the Sturmabteilung, or SA, who provided security at Nazi rallies and disrupted meetings of opposing parties, were likewise empowered. The Gestapo was created soon thereafter.

On February 27, 1933, the Reichstag building—home of the German parliament—burned. This was either a lucky break for Hitler or, perhaps more likely, an event orchestrated by the Nazis themselves. Either way, Hitler blamed the Communists for the blaze. Citing an article of the Weimar Constitution that gave the president license to take emergency measures to ensure public safety and order, Hitler pressured President Hindenburg to issue the Reichstag Fire Decree. This decree suspended certain civil rights, including freedom of the press, freedom of speech, and freedom of assembly. It also suspended the right to privacy, meaning Nazi officials could intercept people's mail, eavesdrop on their phone conversations, and search their homes—all without a warrant. Finally, it granted Hitler's police near-unlimited power of arrest. The Nazis used this decree as the legal basis to imprison their opponents, including the Communists. Those who were arrested were said to be in "protective custody." In reality, that meant they were held indefinitely without trial in makeshift camps around Germany and subjected to great cruelty at the hands of the SA.

Hitler grew yet more powerful after the elections of March 1933, in which the Nazis increased their share of the vote to 43.9 percent. Still, they lacked a majority. To achieve this, Hitler allied with other nationalist parties. Together, Hitler and these allies passed a new law, called the Law for the Relief of the Distress of Nation and State, or, more commonly, the Enabling Act. This law gave the Nazi Party the authority to make laws on their own, without parliamentary approval, granting Hitler unchecked power.

Just two problems remained. First, although it had been defanged, opposition remained. To solve this problem, the

The Nazis used the fire in the Reichstag building in February 1933 for political gains.

Nazis dissolved all other political parties, deemed them illegal, and arrested their leaders. By mid-July 1933, just one legal political party remained in Germany: the Nazi Party. Second, President Hindenburg continued to hold some measure of power. This problem resolved itself in August 1934, when the aged and ailing Hindenburg died. This transpired just one day after Hitler's cabinet enacted a law to abolish the office of the president upon Hindenburg's death and merge its powers with those of the chancellor—Hitler. In this way, Hitler became *Führer und Reichskanzler*—head of the state and head of the government. More importantly, he eradicated the last legal means by which he might be deposed.

The next month, Hitler declared that the Nazi revolution was complete. "There will be no other revolution in Germany for the next one thousand years," he exclaimed. Henceforth, Nazi Germany was often called the Thousand-Year Reich. It was also called the Third Reich. The first *Reich*, or realm, was the Holy Roman Empire. The second was the Hohenzollern dynasty, which ruled Prussia and, later, the German Empire from 1415 to 1918.

Hitler had his eyes on an even bigger prize: dominion over all of Europe—perhaps even the world—and the destruction of an entire people, the Jews.

Lebensraum and the Start of World War II

As far back as the Great War, the Germans had pursued *Lebensraum*, or the expansion of German territory. This was because they believed Germany suffered from three significant disadvantages: its geographic boundaries, inadequate raw materials, and its dense population. By expanding to the east, Germany could become entirely self-sufficient and could develop an economy and standard of living to rival any nation on Earth. As Hitler wrote in *Mein Kampf*, "Germany must find the courage to gather our people, and their strength, for an advance along the road that will lead this people from its present, restricted living-space to new land and soil; and hence also free it from the danger of vanishing from the earth or of serving others as a slave nation."

Obviously, no one was going to simply give Germany this land. The Germans would have to take it. But how?

First, Germany would have to rearm. Nazi leaders called for a standing army of three hundred thousand men by the end of 1937. There was one hitch: the Treaty of Versailles forbade this action. If Germany were to proceed with this plan, it might incite an invasion by neighboring France. To defend against this, German troops reoccupied the Ruhr in 1936. The area had been designated a demilitarized zone following Germany's defeat in the Great War. Incredibly, although the French and the British opposed this action, they did nothing to stop it.

Next, Germany sought to bring other so-called ethnic Germans into the fold, creating a new German Empire. To that end, the Nazis staged a successful coup in neighboring Austria, home of many ethnic Germans, in March 1938—an event called the *Anschluss* (annexation). Hitler then turned his focus to the Sudetenland region of Czechoslovakia, which bordered Austria—also home to many ethnic Germans. This time, rather than staging a coup, Hitler demanded that the Czechoslovakian government grant ethnic Germans in the Sudetenland increased autonomy. The French and British pressured Czechoslovakian president Edvard Beneš to

German troops enter Warsaw, Poland, at the start of World War II in September 1939.

comply. They naïvely believed that appeasing Hitler now would prevent him from seeking yet more territory later. Beneš relented and put forth a plan that bowed to most of Germany's demands. Hitler responded by making new demands—this time to satisfy ethnic claims in Poland and Hungary. In September 1938, Neville Chamberlain, prime minister of Great Britain, asked Hitler for a personal conference. The two met in Munich. There, they signed the Munich Agreement, which handed the Sudetenland over to Germany. Hitler and Chamberlain also signed a peace treaty between their two nations. Back in Britain, Chamberlain boasted that he had achieved "peace for our time." This would prove premature. In March 1939, the German army successfully invaded Prague, the capital of Czechoslovakia, and conquered the rest of the country soon thereafter. Incredibly, this action—like the German reoccupation of the Ruhr—went unchallenged.

At last, the Nazis—emboldened by their successful annexation of Austria and Czechoslovakia—were ready to achieve *Lebensraum* by invading lands to the east. They started with Poland. During the summer of 1939, Hitler hammered out a secret pact with Joseph Stalin, the leader of the Soviet Union, which lay east of Poland. This pact gave Germany free rein to invade Poland. In return, Germany would split the conquered territory with the Soviets.

On September 1, 1939, the Germans invaded Poland. On September 28, as the Germans had predicted, the Poles surrendered. But one thing happened that the Germans *didn't* predict: Britain and France declared war on Germany. This came as a shock. Hitler had believed these two powers would negotiate a settlement after Poland's defeat. Instead, they started World War II.

No matter. Hitler was ready. Indeed, for a time, the Nazis seemed unstoppable. In 1940, they conquered Denmark, Norway, Belgium, the Netherlands, Luxembourg, and France. In 1941, they seized Yugoslavia and Greece. (In spite of Hitler's earlier pact with Stalin, Germany also invaded—but did not conquer—the USSR. It also waged an air war against Great Britain.) Of course, each of these acquisitions became subject to Germany's rule—including the **anti-Semitic** measures it had put in place. This put millions of Jews in grave danger.

TWO

The Indoctrination of the German People

As early as 1922, Hitler told a journalist, "Once I really am in power, my first and foremost task will be the annihilation of the Jews." He promised to hang them indiscriminately "until the last Jew in Munich has been exterminated." He continued, "Other cities will follow suit ... until all Germany has been completely cleansed of the Jews." When Hitler attained the chancellorship in 1933, his views remained unchanged. His methods would differ—rather than being hanged, most Jews would be shot, gassed, or simply worked to death—but he would, indeed, seek to annihilate an entire people.

First, however, he needed to persuade the German populace to go along with his plan. That meant convincing them to share his beliefs about the Jews. To achieve this aim, Hitler passed anti-Semitic laws, distributed anti-Semitic propaganda, censored dissenters, and **indoctrinated** children.

Opposite: Hitler addresses the German people at the Nuremberg Rally of 1935.

A Brief History of Anti-Semitism

Adolf Hitler was hardly the first person to despise the Jews. Indeed, anti-Jew sentiment dates back thousands of years. The early Greeks wrote of the Jews' "ridiculous practices" and the "absurdity of their law." The Romans expelled the Jews from their homeland, in what is modern-day Israel. The Romans also forbade intermarriage between Jews and Christians and barred Jews from various professions. Perhaps even more damaging, the Romans accused the Jews of killing Jesus Christ (who was himself a Jew), when in fact Pontius Pilate, a Roman, had ordered Christ's crucifixion.

Jews faced even harsher measures throughout the Middle Ages. During the Crusades (1095–1291 CE), Christians en route to the Holy Land frequently attacked Jews in Europe, sometimes murdering entire communities. Soon, laws throughout Christendom prevented Jews from owning property, joining trade guilds, or even moving about freely. One right Jews did have, which Christians did not, was to serve as moneylenders and tax collectors. This, however, did not endear them to the Christian populace.

During the twelfth century, an English monk falsely accused the Jews of murdering a Christian child for ritual purposes. Throughout the Middle Ages, Christians leveled similar allegations—now referred to as blood libel—against Jews. According to the Anti-Defamation League, "When a Christian child went missing, it was not uncommon for local Jews to be blamed." Even if there was no evidence against them, "Jews were tortured until they confessed to heinous crimes." Between the twelfth and sixteenth centuries, more than one hundred blood libels occurred, often resulting in the massacre of Jews.

Beginning in the late thirteenth century, the Jews in Europe faced expulsion from their home countries. First, the English expelled the Jews in 1290. France followed suit in 1396, Austria in 1421, Spain in 1492, and Portugal in 1496. Gradually, as more countries in western Europe banished the Jews, many moved eastward. Some went to Holland, known for its religious tolerance. Some landed in Turkey or Palestine, both part of the Ottoman Empire. But most moved to eastern Europe, particularly Poland.

More attacks and expulsions occurred between 1348 and 1354 due to the Black Death. Although rats were in fact to blame, some Europeans believed the Jews were responsible for the plague that killed some twenty-five million people— including, of course, many Jews—over a five-year period. Jews permitted to remain in western Europe after the plague often faced other humiliations. During the sixteenth century, authorities in Venice corralled all the Jews in the city into one small area, which was walled off. Jews were permitted to come and go only at certain times, and were locked in at night. This was the first of many Jewish **ghettos** in Europe.

For a time, it seemed the Jews had a friend in Martin Luther, a key figure in the Protestant Reformation. In 1523, Luther wrote an essay titled *That Jesus Was Born a Jew*, in which he condemned poor treatment of the Jews. Luther's views were grounded on the notion that the Jews could be converted to Christianity. When this proved to be false, Luther's views shifted. In 1543, he published an anti-Jewish treatise called *On the Jews and Their Lies*. This treatise described Jews as a "base, whoring people" who were "full of the devil's feces." Christians, he said, should set fire to their synagogues, schools, and homes; confiscate their property and money; destroy their prayer books; and afford them no legal protection. The Jews—whom Luther described as "poisonous envenomed worms"—should be expelled, forced into labor, or even murdered. "We are at fault in not slaying them," he wrote.

The advent of the Enlightenment, in the eighteenth century, brought new ideals such as brotherhood, progress, liberty, and tolerance. During this period, Jews played a full part in European society—at least in some places. They could live where they wanted, go to school where they wished, and enter whatever profession they liked. Many Jews assumed important roles in the arts, politics, science, and business.

In 1789, during the French Revolution, France's National Assembly passed the Declaration of the Rights of Man and of the Citizen, further strengthening the position of the Jews. This important document guaranteed freedom of religion and recognized the equality of all citizens—including Jews—under the law. These ideals soon spread beyond France as Emperor Napoleon Bonaparte conquered vast areas of Europe, including Italy, the Netherlands, and Germany.

Sadly, these freedoms were short-lived. After the fall of Napoleon in 1815, many countries revoked the rights of the Jews. According to author Amos Elon, some areas in Germany went so far as to "return Jews to their old medieval status." Elon explained, "The free city of Frankfurt reinstated parts of the medieval statute that restricted the rights of Jews. As in 1616, only twelve Jewish couples were allowed to marry each year." Elon continued, "The 400,000 gulden the [Jewish] community had paid the city government in 1811 in return for its emancipation were declared forfeited." And, he said, "In the Rhineland ... Jews lost the citizenship rights they had been granted under the French and were no longer allowed to practice certain professions. The few who had been appointed to public office before the war were summarily dismissed." **Pogroms** soon followed, during which many Jews were murdered and their property ruined.

Soon, the Germans would develop a "scientific" reason for their hatred of the Jews. Jews, they believed, were an inferior race. One German leader, Hermann Ahlwardt, likened Jews to "cholera bacilli" and called for their extermination in 1895. Another, Heinrich Class, insisted German Jews be stripped of their citizenship and forbidden to own land, hold public office, or participate in various professions, such as journalism and banking.

During this period, anti-Jewish newspapers,

The Nazis taught their "scientific" reasons for the inferiority of the Jews in schools.

journals, and pamphlets flourished. In 1879, a German journalist named Wilhelm Marr, who coined the term anti-Semite to describe a person who is prejudiced against Jews, penned a pamphlet titled *The Way to Victory of Germanism over Judaism.* This pamphlet claimed that the Germans and Jews were locked in "a perpetual racial conflict." Worse, given the inroads made by Jews in finance, industry, and professional life, the Germans were losing. If the Jews prevailed, claimed Marr, the result would be *finis Germaniae*—the end of the German people. Only by destroying the Jews, said Marr, could Germany survive. To that end, he founded the League of Anti-Semites, "committed to combatting the danger presented by a Jewish race."

These offenses did not go entirely unnoticed. As German philosopher Friedrich Nietzsche observed in 1886, "The whole problem of the Jews exists only in nation states, for here their energy and higher intelligence, their accumulated capital of spirit and will, gathered from generation to generation through a long schooling in suffering, must become so preponderant as to arouse mass envy and hatred." Nietzsche continued, "In almost all contemporary nations, therefore—in direct proportion to the degree to which they act up nationalistically—the literal obscenity of leading the Jews to slaughter as scapegoats for every conceivable public and internal misfortune is spreading."

Even Jews who managed to migrate from Europe, such as the 1.75 million Jews who moved to the United States between 1900 and 1920, faced prejudice—especially as their numbers grew. Groups like the Immigration Restriction

League argued that these Jews were "culturally, intellectually, morally and biologically inferior." And yet, despite these perceived shortcomings, many Americans also believed the Jews controlled both Washington and Wall Street.

The Jews were no strangers to prejudice and oppression. But even they could never have imagined the level of anti-Semitism in Nazi Germany. Hitler and the Nazi Party sought to systematically wipe the Jews off the face of the earth … and they very nearly succeeded.

Anti-Semitic Laws

Despite a history of German anti-Semitism, most Jews in Germany were proud German citizens. Germany was their home. They spoke the German language. German Jews made significant contributions to German society. They held important posts in the German government. They taught at top German universities. Between 1905 and 1936, German Jews received fourteen Nobel Prizes. During the Great War, more than one hundred thousand Jews served in the German military. Many were decorated for their courage. Many German Jews had assimilated into German society to such a degree that they married non-Jews.

Starting in March 1933, life for Jews in Germany changed. Nazis began attacking Jewish businesses and synagogues, as well as Jews simply going about their business around town. Many Jews were beaten or even killed. Hitler no doubt approved of the sentiment behind these actions. The methods, however, were another matter. Hitler realized that the chaos wrought by these assaults damaged the German

Nazis outside Woolworths encourage a boycott of the business in 1933. (Woolworths was not founded by Jews, as these Nazis believed, but by a pair of Methodists.)

economy. Moreover, the attacks, which occurred in a random manner, were outside the purview of the state. Far better, Hitler thought, to pass anti-Semitic legislation. Then, ever so slowly, he could turn up the heat, solving the "Jewish problem" once and for all.

On the Saturday before Easter in 1933, one of the best business days of the year, the Nazis organized a nationwide boycott of Jewish-owned businesses. Members of the SA and SS stood outside Jewish-owned businesses throughout Germany, hurling abuse at any customers who dared to enter. Some carried signs. One such sign, displayed outside Israel's Department Store in Berlin, read, "Germans! Defend Yourselves! Don't Buy from Jews!" That wasn't all. Nazis scrawled the word *Jude* (Jew) across many shop windows and painted a yellow and black **Star of David** on many shop doors. Some Nazis marched through town chanting anti-Semitic slogans and singing pro-Nazi songs. In some areas of Germany, violence erupted. One Jew, a lawyer in Kiel, was murdered. Although the state-sponsored boycott ended after just one day, members of the SA continued to harass and attack Jews and to boycott their businesses on an "unofficial" basis. Inevitably, due to these and other conditions, Jewish businesses lost customers.

Just days after the April boycott, the Nazis passed the first of some two thousand anti-Semitic laws, decrees, and orders. Called the Law for the Restoration of the Professional Civil Service, this law dictated that Jews be removed from the civil service and replaced by Aryan workers. (Jews who were veterans of the Great War were exempt from these restrictions—though not for long.)

That same year, the Nazis passed many other restrictive orders. The Law Concerning Admission to the Legal Profession prevented Jewish lawyers entrance into the bar and prohibited those already in the bar from practicing their profession. Similarly, the Law Concerning Admission to the Medical Profession barred Jewish doctors from practicing in hospitals. Later, the Nazis would ban Jewish doctors from treating non-Jews. By the end of 1933, Jews were no longer eligible to work as journalists, nor were Jews permitted to own farmland or engage in agriculture.

In September 1935, the Nazis tightened the screws with the passage of two more anti-Semitic laws. They introduced these new laws at an annual rally held in Nuremberg; hence,

Attacking the Weak

During this period, the Germans also passed laws that negatively affected other groups. One such law was the Law for the Prevention of Hereditarily Diseased Offspring, sometimes called the Sterilization Law. This law, passed in July 1933, called for the sterilization of anyone suffering from a hereditary disease. The list of applicable diseases included congenital mental deficiency, schizophrenia, manic depression, hereditary epilepsy, hereditary chorea, hereditary blindness, hereditary deafness, and any severe hereditary deformity. Those suffering from alcoholism were also subject to sterilization.

A similar law, the Law Against Dangerous Habitual Criminals, passed two years later. Under this law, criminals were sterilized. This law was also used as the legal basis for the imprisonment of "social misfits"—the unemployed, prostitutes, beggars, alcoholics, vagrants, and Roma people.

they are called the Nuremberg Laws. One law was the Law for the Protection of German Blood and Honor. This law forbade Jews from marrying or having sexual relations with members of the Aryan race—a practice called *rassenschande*, or "racial defilement." Later, this law would be extended to include even nonsexual forms of contact, such as a kiss in greeting or a friendly embrace. The law also forbade the employment of German women under the age of forty-five in Jewish homes.

The second law was the Reich Citizenship Law. It stripped the Jews of their German citizenship and all accompanying legal rights. This was even more troublesome, as it paved the way for yet more radical laws against the Jews, like the 1936 law that forbade Jews from frequenting public parks and swimming pools. That same year, the Nazis also banned Jews from owning equipment, typewriters, or bicycles; from working as tax agents, tax advisors, or veterinarians; or voting in government elections. In 1937, the Nazis declared Jewish passports invalid for foreign travel.

The year 1938 saw yet more restrictive anti-Semitic laws. That year, the Nazis required all Jews to register property in excess of a specified amount. They also required the registration and identification of all Jewish businesses. (This information was no doubt useful to the Nazis when, in November 1938, they issued a decree forcing all Jews to transfer their retail establishments to Aryans.) To limit their movement, the Nazis expressly prohibited the Jews from traveling freely about the country, owning a car, or possessing a driver's license, and they imposed a curfew. Later, Jews would be forbidden even from using public transportation. Cinemas, theaters, and sports facilities were likewise *verboten*. Adding insult to injury, the Nazis even replaced Jewish street names with German ones.

To prevent the dissemination of information to the Jewish populace, the Nazis mandated that all Jews surrender their radios to the police in 1939. In 1941, they banned Jews from using any public library. And in 1942, they forbade Jews from subscribing to newspapers or magazines. The Nazis likewise sought to limit the spread of information by

Jews among themselves, declaring in 1940 that Jews were no longer permitted to install, maintain, or use a telephone in their home or, later, to use public telephones. Even the use of carrier pigeons was off limits. In time, Jews would be forbidden to own pets, visit barbershops, own fur coats or woolen clothing, possess gemstones or precious metals (although the Nazis did permit Jews to keep one silver place setting each), or buy basic necessities such as meat, eggs, and milk.

The Jews suffered yet another notable indignity under the Nazis. Starting in September 1941, the Nazis forced all German Jews over the age of six to wear a yellow Star of David sewn on their clothing as an identifying badge. Similar rules also applied to Jews in territories conquered by Germany. Anyone caught not wearing their badge risked severe punishment—including death. The next year, the Germans dictated that all Jews mark the entrance to their homes with a black Star of David. Because Jews were now visually identifiable, they faced increasing verbal and physical assaults from the German public, which—thanks to Nazi propaganda—now viewed Jews as subhuman.

All told, between 1933 and 1942, the Nazis succeeded in stripping German Jews of their work, their social standing and role in society, their dignity, and in many cases, their lives.

Anti-Semitic Propaganda

How did the Nazis convince the German populace—and later, people in the areas they conquered—that the Jews were their enemy? In large part, they achieved this through the careful use of propaganda.

Who Was "Jewish"?

According to the Nuremberg Laws, a Jew was not a person with a specific set of religious beliefs. Rather, a Jew was anyone with at least three Jewish grandparents. This was true even if the person had given up Judaism, had never practiced it, or had converted to another religion, like Christianity.

What about someone with one or two Jewish grandparents? The Nazis called such a person *Mischling*, or "mixed blood." Someone with two Jewish grandparents was called Mischling of the first degree. Someone with just one Jewish grandparent was called Mischling of the second degree. *Mischlinge* (plural of Mischling) of the second degree were eligible for German citizenship, although they were not considered "pure." The same was true of Mischlinge of the first degree unless they practiced Judaism; were married to a Jew (in which case their children would also be Jewish); were born after September 17, 1935, to at least one Jewish parent; or were born out of wedlock to at least one Jewish parent after July 31, 1936. In those cases, Mischlinge of the first degree were classified as Jewish under the law.

After their ascent to power, the Nazis quickly took control of all forms of mass communication in Germany. This effort was led by the Reich Ministry for Popular Entertainment and Propaganda, headed by Dr. Joseph Goebbels. Goebbels sought to control what the German people read, saw, and heard. Key to their effort was repetition. As Hitler himself wrote in *Mein Kampf*, "The chief function of propaganda is to convince the masses, whose slowness of understanding needs to be given time so they may absorb information; and only constant repetition will finally succeed in imprinting an idea on their mind."

Nazi propaganda wasn't intended to incite violence against the Jews outright. Rather, it sought to depict Jews as subhuman, such that if Jews *were* attacked, Germans would not regard it as a crime. As noted by scholar Caesar C. Aronsfeld, "The incessant propaganda created, and was intended to create, an atmosphere in which the murder of the Jews was to be regarded as not only not a crime but, on the contrary, as a meritorious deed performed in the service of the human race." Thanks to Nazi propaganda, the extermination of the Jews moved from ideology to action.

One common form of propaganda was anti-Semitic newspapers. The first and perhaps most virulent of these was *Der Stürmer* (the *Storm Trooper*), published by Julius Streicher. Streicher frequently called for the annihilation of the Jews in the pages of his newspaper. One famous issue, published in 1939, featured on its front page a medieval image of Jews performing a ritual murder—a modern example of blood libel. Other issues accused Jews of being warmongers and of destroying the social order. Even the newspaper's office featured an offensive caricature of a Jew in its front window.

Posters were another common form of propaganda. The Nazis displayed these anywhere they could. These posters

A man reads outside the offices of *Der Stürmer*, one of Nazi Germany's most virulent anti-Semitic newspapers.

typically blamed the Jews for Germany's problems, depicting them in a rudely stereotypical manner. In one poster, a large hand points to a cowering Jew, flanked by the words "He is guilty for the war!" In another, a Jewish man hides behind British, American, and Soviet flags, with the words "Behind the enemy powers: the Jews."

The Nazis didn't just use print propaganda, however. Radio was another important medium. Indeed, Hitler pushed for the development and manufacture of a cheap and accessible radio, called the VE 301, very early in his reign. He wanted all Germans to own one so they could listen to propaganda broadcasts. By 1938, nearly 70 percent of Germans who lived in the cities owned a VE 301. And after the introduction of an even cheaper version the next year, radio ownership—in the city and the countryside— almost doubled. Using their radios, Germans could listen in on Nazi rallies and on political speeches by Hitler and other high-ranking Nazis. Because these radios offered no shortwave capabilities, listening to foreign broadcasts was impossible—and eventually, illegal.

Films, too, were an effective form of propaganda. Indeed, both Hitler and Goebbels believed film was an essential tool for molding public opinion. For this reason, the Nazis released many documentary-style films. Some of these films were meant to raise up Hitler, the Nazi Party, and the Aryan ideal. An example of this type of film was *Der Sieg des Glaubens* (*The Victory of Faith*), which depicted a Nazi rally that occurred in September 1933. Another was *Triumph des Willens* (*Triumph of the Will*), which chronicled a Nazi gathering attended by some seven hundred thousand supporters, complete with rousing speeches by key Nazi leaders, including Hitler. A famous female filmmaker named Leni Riefenstahl directed and produced both of these films.

Other propaganda films were meant to denigrate Jews. Perhaps the most famous of these was *Der Ewige Jude* (*The Eternal Jew*), made in 1940. The goal of this film was to completely dehumanize the Jews. According to the film, Jews were nothing more than rats. As noted by the film's narrator, "Among the animals, [rats] represent the rudiment of an insidious, underground destruction—just like the Jews among human beings." But unlike rats, the film claimed, Jews had an uncanny ability to blend in with their "human hosts." In other words, the Jews were not the civilized Europeans they appeared to be. Rather, their natural state was that of the dirty, unshaven, and unkempt Jews found in the Polish ghettos. The film went on to blame the Jews for Germany's woes, including inflation and unemployment, before closing

GROSSE POLITISCHE SCHAU IN DER NORDWESTBAHNHALLE IN WIEN. AB 30. JULI 1938. TÄGLICH GEÖFFNET VON 10-20 UHR

A movie poster for *Der Ewige Jude* (*The Eternal Jew*). Notice the stereotypical depiction of the Jewish man.

with footage of an anti-Semitic speech by Hitler and images of a procession of SA troops. According to scholar Stephen Fritz, *Der Ewige Jude* served as "both a demonstration of the parasitical nature of the Jews and a justification for drastic measures against them." Another scholar, Maria Tatar, noted that the film was meant to "position the victims of [the Nazis'] genocidal project as dangerous aggressors who had to be exterminated." Finally, Richard Barsam described the film as a call to kill Jews, noting that in Nazi Germany, "killing them is not a crime, but a necessity—just as killing rats is a necessity to preserve health and cleanliness."

Censorship

The Nazis used propaganda to spread their viewpoint, but they didn't stop there. They also used censorship to suppress the viewpoints of those who disagreed with them, and to prevent Germans from discovering information that might compromise the nation, the party, or the war effort in general. In other words, the Nazis used censorship to hide the truth. All media were subject to censorship, including newspapers, literature, and music—even public events. The Nazis even tried to censor personal communications, such as mail and private conversations, but this effort was less successful.

As part of their censorship activities, the Nazis conducted book burnings. The first of these occurred in the spring of 1933. Professors and librarians who had been swayed by the Nazi ideology compiled a long list of books not suitable for reading by Germans—that is, books that contradicted Nazi beliefs in any way. Then, on the night of May 10, Nazis

The Distortion of Language

While it's true that the Nazis worked to ensure that the German citizens turned their backs on the Jews, they also wanted to conceal the true nature of their activities: the deportation and brutal murder of millions of Jews. To achieve this, they chose their words very carefully. For example, German officials didn't use the word "genocide"; they said "cleansing" or "thinning out." Rather than "deportation," they said "resettlement" or "evacuation." Rather than "gas chamber," they said "bath arrangements." And those killed weren't "victims"; they were "figures" or "pieces." In this way, the Nazis enabled the German people to distance themselves from the horrors wrought upon the Jews.

in Berlin ransacked libraries and bookstores for these titles, which they carted to a bonfire in the city's Opera Square. After a speech by Goebbels, in which he condemned works by "un-German" writers, including Jews, liberals, leftists, pacifists, and foreigners, the books were burned—an act that Goebbels described as the "cleansing of the German spirit."

The book burning wasn't limited to just Berlin, however; that same night, thousands of books were burned nationwide. Some of these were works by Jews, such as Albert Einstein and Sigmund Freud. Others were by Americans, including Ernest Hemingway, Sinclair Lewis, and Jack London. The

Nazis even burned books by Helen Keller. (When told of this insult, Keller replied, "Tyranny cannot defeat the power of ideas.")

The Indoctrination of Children

As part of their attempt to ensure total compliance among the German population both then and in the future, the Nazis took special care to indoctrinate children with the party's ideology.

One tactic was to publish children's books, primers, and even coloring books that promoted anti-Semitism, obedience to the Nazi Party, and a love for Hitler. One such book was *Trau Keinem Fuchs auf Grüner Heid und Keinem Jud Bei Seinem Eid (Trust No Fox in the Green Meadow and No Jew on His Oath)*. In this book, the Jew is depicted in a stereotypically negative fashion. In contrast, the German

A group of young German girls greet their Führer.

children shown in the book look healthy, happy, and hale. In another book, similar illustrations are accompanied by derogatory text, such as "Jews are our misfortune" and "How the Jew cheats."

Another approach was to form Nazi organizations specifically for children. Younger boys, ages ten to fourteen, joined the Young German Folk, while older boys, ages fourteen to eighteen, joined the Hitler Youth. These groups met after school to develop their physical fitness. Girls had similar options. The *Jungmädel* (Young Girls League) served girls ages ten to fourteen, while the *Bund Deutscher Mädel* (League of German Girls) catered to girls fourteen to eighteen. They, too, met to develop their physical fitness, as well as attend classes in homemaking. All four organizations were intended to indoctrinate members—who were made to swear an oath of love and loyalty to Hitler—in Nazi ideology and to train them to be good Aryans. Of course, they permitted no Jews to join.

And of course, the Nazi Party used schools to spread their ideas. This was made easier by the fact that many teachers joined the Nazi Party, and even taught school while wearing a Nazi uniform. Soon, German teachers did more than educate students on traditional subjects such as reading, writing, and arithmetic. They also began instructing pupils on the principles of racial purity. Often, this meant calling Jewish children to the front of the room to serve as examples of "non-Aryans." These children were frequently subjected to additional humiliations, such as the teacher pointing to their eyes, ears, nose, mouth, and hair, and comparing them with the features of Aryan children.

Inevitably, Jewish children found themselves the target of verbal and physical abuse by their teachers and their fellow students. But in time, this would stop—but only because Jewish children were banned from attending German schools in 1938. Instead, they studied at segregated schools of their own. In 1942, even those segregated schools were closed.

No Escape

The Nazis sought the annihilation of the Jews. For a time, however, the party might have been satisfied with all German Jews simply leaving Germany. Indeed, between 1933 and 1941, the Nazis sought to become *judenrein* (cleansed of the Jews) by making life so miserable and impossible for German Jews that they would move elsewhere of their own volition. To that end, the Nazis passed the laws and disseminated the propaganda described in this chapter.

At the same time, the Nazis made it very difficult for Jews to leave, forcing any Jew who emigrated to surrender as much as 90 percent of his or her wealth or risk imprisonment. There was one exception, however: Jews bound for Palestine—then a British territory—were permitted to transfer a portion of their assets abroad. As a result, some sixty thousand German Jews sought refuge in Palestine following the ascension of the Nazis in 1933. Unfortunately for the Jews, this avenue of escape narrowed after the 1936–1939 Arab Revolt, during which Palestinian Arabs rose up against British rule. In 1939, the British—wary of creating yet more upheaval—severely

Why Palestine?

Until the second century CE, Jews lived in the area that by 1933 was named Palestine. It was their homeland. In 63 BCE, after the Siege of Jerusalem, the Romans conquered the Jews, claiming their land. The Jews did not want to live under Roman rule, however. They rebelled the first time in 66 CE and were defeated four years later. They rebelled again between 132 and 136 CE. In retaliation, the Romans executed thousands of Jews and sold the rest into slavery. Any Jew who somehow escaped these two fates had no choice but to flee. This event, scholars say, marks the beginning of the Jewish diaspora—a term that describes the expulsion of Jews from their homeland and their subsequent dispersal across the world, including Europe.

restricted the flow of Jewish refugees into Palestine. This policy would remain in place until 1948.

The German Jews faced yet another problem: most other countries maintained immigration quotas and were unwilling to ease them to let in more Jews. For example, in the United States, many Americans—themselves in the midst of the Great Depression—were disinclined to admit Jewish refugees. They feared these incoming Jews would compete for jobs, which were scarce, and would overload social programs, which were already overtaxed. No doubt, widespread anti-Semitism and xenophobia among both the US public and government officials were also a factor.

In 1938, thirty-two countries sent delegates to an international conference held in Évian-les-Bains, France, to discuss the plight of Germany's Jews. Delegate after delegate conveyed their sympathy for these oppressed people, but few offered practical solutions. France and the United States refused to ease their immigration restrictions, citing economic problems and population levels. The British did one better: not only did they refuse to allow more Jewish refugees to immigrate, they apologized to the German government for having interfered on the issue. Australia, too, declined to help, explaining that "as we have no real racial problem, we are not desirous of importing one." In the end, only one country represented at the conference, the Dominican Republic, offered to accept more refugees—as many as one hundred thousand—albeit in exchange for a significant sum. (In fact, only eight hundred refugees entered the tiny island country, most of whom then hopped over to the nearby US.) Hitler declared it "astounding" that these countries did not hesitate to criticize Germany's treatment of the Jews, but refused to open their own doors when "the opportunity offer[ed]."

Not even the plight of Jewish children moved these foreign governments to act. In February 1939, Senator Robert F. Wagner (Democrat from New York) and Representative Edith Nourse Rogers (Republican from Massachusetts) introduced the Wagner-Rogers refugee aid bill. This bill allowed for the admission of twenty thousand German refugee children into the United States. Incredibly, Congress defeated the bill.

Not everyone turned their backs, however. Between 1933 and 1941, the city of Shanghai, China, took in more than eighteen thousand Jewish refugees. Between 1938 and 1941, Bolivia issued some twenty thousand visas to European Jews. And unlike the US, which refused to aid Jewish children, Great Britain allowed thousands of these young refugees from Germany, Austria, Czechoslovakia, and Poland to enter the country between 1938 and 1948—a rescue operation popularly referred to as the Kindertransport.

In the end, the issue was moot. Starting in 1941, it became illegal for Jews to emigrate from Germany. Many Jews who had remained in Germany or in countries conquered by Hitler's forces would become victims of one of the worst acts of genocide in human history.

THREE

The Nazi Terror

Having passed the necessary laws to terrorize the Jews— and having distributed the necessary propaganda to ensure the majority of the German populace would not only allow but engage in this endeavor—the Nazis were primed to enter a new phase. During this period, which commenced in 1938 and continued until the end of World War II, Jews were not merely harassed or attacked on a random basis. Rather, they became the targets of a systematic effort to annihilate them.

November 9–10, 1938, represented a turning point in Nazi Germany. On the night of the ninth, anti-Jewish riots erupted all over Germany.

What prompted the unrest? Supposedly, it was the death of a German diplomat, who had been shot by a Jew in Paris. According to German propaganda, this incited the citizens of Germany to rise up. However, this did not happen by accident. After the diplomat's death, Propaganda Minister Goebbels was careful to say that "The Führer has decided that ... demonstrations should not be prepared or

Opposite: Germans survey Jewish businesses damaged during Kristallnacht.

organized by the party." But, he continued, "insofar as they erupt spontaneously, they are not to be hampered." This was a clear signal to party leaders to organize a pogrom—so they did.

Starting around 10:30 p.m., regional party leaders and members of Hitler's SA and SS donned civilian clothes, armed themselves with axes and sledgehammers, and stormed the streets all over Germany. Together, these thugs demolished nearly every synagogue in Germany—some 250 in all—and every prayer book, scroll, and piece of artwork within them. (Interestingly, they stole synagogue archives rather than destroying them. Instead, they gave them to the Sicherheitsdienst, or SD, which was the intelligence arm of the SS.) They vandalized Jewish cemeteries, uprooting headstones and desecrating graves. They ruined more than seven thousand Jewish businesses and ransacked Jewish homes. They detained more than thirty thousand Jewish men, who were later sent to forced-labor camps. And they beat nearly one hundred Jews to death. Later, this event would be dubbed Kristallnacht (Night of the Broken Glass). This referred to the shards of glass that littered the streets after the riots, thanks to the Nazi brutes who had shattered the windows of Jewish stores, homes, hospitals, schools, and synagogues.

One British reporter, Hugh Greene of the *Daily Telegraph*, described the pogrom in an article published November 11. "Mob law ruled in Berlin throughout the afternoon and evening and hordes of hooligans indulged in an orgy of destruction," he wrote. "I have seen several anti-Jewish outbreaks in Germany during the last five years, but never anything as nauseating as this." Greene continued, "Racial hatred and hysteria seemed to have taken complete hold of otherwise decent people. I saw fashionably dressed women clapping their hands and screaming with glee, while respectable middle-class mothers held up their babies to see the 'fun.'"

Not all Germans approved of this pogrom, however. Indeed, many German people found it abhorrent. As observed by William Dodd, then the US ambassador to Germany, "In view of this being a totalitarian state a surprising characteristic of the situation here is the intensity and scope among German citizens of condemnation of the recent happenings against Jews." (In response to growing unrest in Germany, the US government soon called Dodd home.) The vast majority of police and firefighters simply stood by during the riots, but some did attempt to help Jews under attack. Even some Nazi troops and Hitler Youth voiced their disgust, openly refusing party orders to participate in the destruction.

Nevertheless, the tenor of anti-Jewish persecution had changed literally overnight. No longer were the Jews subjected to mere harassment, economic hardship, and the occasional attack. Now, they faced beatings, imprisonment, and even murder. Indeed, it was this event, Kristallnacht, that marked the start of the Holocaust.

Ghettos

Following Germany's invasion of Poland in 1939, the Nazis rounded up large numbers of Polish Jews and confined them in what they called "Jewish residential quarters"—a nice way of saying "ghettos." The Jews could bring with them

Exported Pogroms

Kristallnacht was just one of many pogroms instigated by the Nazis—although many of these other pogroms occurred outside of Germany and were perpetrated by local residents. During the Iaşi pogrom, in Romania, townspeople and police killed as many as fourteen thousand Romanian Jews. In the Lviv pogroms, in a region of Poland that would become part of Ukraine, Ukrainian nationalists murdered some six thousand Polish Jews. And in Jedwabne, also in Poland, local Poles burned some three hundred Jews to death in a locked barn. These are just a few of the pogroms that occurred.

only those belongings they could carry themselves. Later, the Nazis would transport thousands of German and Austrian Jews to these ghettos. The Nazis put these Jews to work to support the German war effort.

Typically, Jewish ghettos—all told, there were at least a thousand, first in Poland and later in the USSR—were bound by high walls or fences with barbed wire. German guards manned all entrances and exits. Jews were prevented not just from leaving, but from having any contact with the outside world.

Jewish ghettos were, in the words of scholar Erik Barnouw, "pockets of indescribable misery." Simply put, life in the ghetto was unbearable. Overcrowding was common. For example, in the Warsaw ghetto, the Nazis crammed more than four hundred thousand Jews into an area of just 1.3 square miles (3.4 square kilometers). Apartments that once housed a single family now held several. Many of these apartments lacked running water. Sanitation facilities were primitive at best. Hunger was rampant. In an attempt to starve ghetto residents, the Nazis restricted food rations, allowing only small amounts of bread, potatoes, and fat. Heating fuel was likewise scarce—a problem compounded by the fact that many residents lacked warm clothing. Not surprisingly, hundreds of thousands of Jews died in the ghettos. Some died of exposure. Others perished from starvation. Still others fell prey to disease, such as typhoid. Some Jews in the ghettos committed suicide simply to escape their misery.

Orphaned children were common in Jewish ghettos. Many of these had no alternative but to beg in the streets. Countless died. Still, many children showed remarkable resilience in the face of extreme hardship. At great personal risk, children often crawled through narrow gaps in the ghetto wall to obtain food, which they smuggled back in. To entertain themselves, they made toys of discarded cloth or wood. In one ghetto, children made playing cards from cigarette box tops.

For each ghetto, the Nazis installed a *Judenrat* (Jewish council). These councils took their orders from the SS. The Judenrat, typically composed of influential Jews within the community, was responsible for the day-to-day operation of the ghetto. For example, it was the job of the Judenrat to distribute whatever limited food, water, and heating oil was available. Far more difficult for the Judenrat was the

Hungry Jewish children sit outside a food shop in the Warsaw ghetto.

task of confiscating property from Jews in the ghetto and providing workers for forced labor. Later, the Judenrat would be given an even harder job: selecting Jews to be deported to **extermination camps**. Any council members who refused to comply were shot.

Death Squads

With the German invasion of the Soviet Union in June 1941 came a new stage in the Holocaust. Jews were no longer simply rounded up and herded into ghettos. Now, they were murdered on sight. These murders were performed by special SS units called *Einsatzgruppen*.

In essence, the Einsatzgruppen were mobile death squads. They moved in the wake of the German army as it advanced through the USSR. Any Jews the Einsatzgruppen discovered in German-occupied territory—men, women, children, infants, the elderly—they killed. Often, they did so with the aid of local residents.

When the Einsatzgruppen entered a town or city, they rounded up all Jewish residents. Then they forced these Jews to hand over any valuables. They also made the Jews take off their clothes, which were often distributed to local collaborators. Next, the Einsatzgruppen marched the Jews to

A memorial honors the children killed during the slaughter at Babi Yar.

a field, forest, or ravine on the outskirts of town. There, the Einsatzgruppen usually did one of two things: they shot the Jews to death or they shoved them into gas vans, which were mobile gas chambers. Finally, they dumped the victims' bodies into a mass grave.

The worst of these massacres occurred at Babi Yar, near Kiev. There, nearly thirty-four thousand Jews were murdered in groups of ten over the course of two days in September 1941. According to the book *The World Must Know: The History of the Holocaust as Told in the United States Holocaust Memorial Museum*, a witness to the event described the scene. "They were led into the ravine, which was about 150 meters [500 feet] long and 30 meters [100 ft] wide and a good 15 meters [50 ft] deep," the witness said. "When they reached the bottom of the ravine, they were seized by members of the *Schutzpolizei* [armed police force] and made to lie down on top of Jews who had already been shot. The corpses were literally in layers." The witness continued, "A police marksman came along and shot each Jew in the neck with a submachine gun." All told, the Einsatzgruppen murdered more than a million Jews between 1941 and 1943.

The Final Solution

No doubt, Jewish ghettos and mobile death squads offered an effective way to exterminate Jews. Still, the Nazis weren't satisfied. They sought a more efficient solution to what they called the Jewish question.

In January 1942, Reinhard Heydrich, head deputy to SS chief Heinrich Himmler, convened a meeting at a villa by Lake Wannsee, on the outskirts of Berlin. The purpose of this meeting, later called the Wannsee Conference, was not to conceive of a solution to the Jewish question. That had already been done. Rather, the meeting was called to outline that plan—called *die Endlösung der Judenfrage* (the Final Solution to the Jewish Question)—to the heads of various governmental departments and to ensure their cooperation.

So what was the plan? Simply put, it was to deport every Jew in Europe to extermination camps. At these camps, located in occupied Poland, each one of these Jews would be murdered. Incredibly, not a single meeting attendee—there were fifteen in all—voiced opposition to this course of action.

Although they had let these senior government officials in on the plot, the Nazis sought to keep this information from the German people. As Himmler said during a speech in 1943, "The hard decision had to be made that this people should be caused to disappear from the earth." He continued, "Perhaps, at a much later time, we can consider whether we should say something more about this to the German people." Then he reconsidered: "I myself believe that it is better for us—us together—to have borne this for our people, that we have taken the responsibility for it on ourselves (the responsibility for an act, not just for an idea), and that we should now take this secret with us to the grave." It seems that Himmler equated the Nazis' silence about this mass murder with heroism and sacrifice.

Deportations Begin

Within months, the Nazis commenced with their plan. Jews were transported, usually by train, to one of six extermination camps in occupied Poland: Auschwitz-Birkenau, Chełmno, Bełzec, Majdanek, Sobibór, or Treblinka. First came the Jews from the ghettos in the east. Then came Jews from

Hungarian Jews arrive at the Auschwitz extermination camp, circa 1942, which was early in the period of mass killings.

Types of Nazi Camps

Although many people use the terms interchangeably, extermination camps were different from concentration camps.

From the start of their rule, the Nazis had used **concentration camps**—so named because they *concentrated* prisoners in one place—to detain political opponents, such as communists, without trial. In time, all manner of "undesirables" were imprisoned in these camps, including Jews. For example, the thirty thousand Jews arrested on Kristallnacht were sent to concentration camps. In fact, by 1940, it became the German policy to deport all Jews to concentration camps (or, as the Nazis euphemistically and ironically called it, to place them in "protective custody"). Concentration camps—such as Dachau, built in 1933; Mauthausen, built in 1938; and Ravensbrück, built in 1939—were not intended to be killing centers per se. The purpose of these camps was to terrorize anyone who refused to conform. Still, due to camp conditions, many prisoners died in concentration camps.

In contrast, extermination camps, also called death camps, were designed for the express purpose of murdering all who entered them, usually as soon as they arrived.

In addition to extermination camps and concentration camps, the Nazis built transit camps, such as Drancy in France and Westerbork in the Netherlands. These camps served as way stations for prisoners bound for concentration camps or extermination camps. The Nazis also built forced-labor camps, where they subjected inmates to "extermination through labor." In concentration camps, prisoners were forced to work for the war effort, and often died as a result—but their death was incidental. In forced-labor camps, however, prisoners were forced to work *so that they would die*. Interestingly, many forced-labor camps operated in partnership with various private German businesses, including Messerschmidt, Junkers, Siemens, IG Farben, and even BMW.

In all, the Nazis built more than twenty thousand camps of these four varieties.

concentration camps in Germany and in various other conquered lands—France, Belgium, the Netherlands, Norway, Hungary, Romania, Italy, Greece, and North Africa.

En route, these Jews were subjected to appalling conditions. Typically, they were crammed into train cars meant for animals. One survivor recalled, "There is no room to sit. In order to make room we are forced to stand with our hands above our heads." Some of the train cars were open at the top, exposing passengers to cold and rain. Perhaps even worse, however, were the cars that were closed. In these cars, the prisoners were left in darkness, with little air. They received little food or water. The train cars had no sanitation facilities; instead, prisoners were forced to use buckets.

For many, the journey took days. Not surprisingly, numerous prisoners—particularly the very young, the very old, and the sick—died along the way.

Arriving at the Extermination Camp

Some extermination camp complexes also housed a concentration camp and/or a forced-labor camp. One such complex was Auschwitz, a 19-square-mile (50-sq km) complex located near the Polish town of Oswiecim. Auschwitz I, the main camp, was a concentration camp. It opened in 1940. In 1941, the Germans began construction on Auschwitz II, also called Auschwitz-Birkenau. This was an extermination camp. Finally, in 1942, Auschwitz III, also known as Buna or Monowitz, opened. A forced-labor camp, it provided workers for a rubber factory.

Upon their arrival at a camp complex like Auschwitz, camp guards ordered those Jews who had survived the journey by train to disembark. Next, they told the arriving prisoners to form two lines—men in one and women and children in the other. The prisoners were then subject to a selection process. A Nazi official briefly examined each person to determine whether he or she might be spared for labor. Then he instructed the person to stand to the left or to the right. Those in one group would live and those in the other would die. Roughly 80 percent of these new arrivals—particularly the very young, very old, infirm, or pregnant—landed in the group bound for death.

Sometimes, those condemned to die—whether at a camp like Auschwitz, where they had been marked for death during the selection process, or at a camp like Treblinka, where often, no such selection even took place—were shot. More often, they were led to a gas chamber—although they didn't know that. Usually, the guards told the prisoners it was a shower. After instructing the prisoners to turn over their valuables and to take off their clothes, the guards prodded them into the chamber, locked the doors, and piped in the gas. Sometimes they employed carbon monoxide. Other times it was Zyklon-B, a cyanide gas originally developed to exterminate insects. Within minutes, the prisoners were dead.

After the poisonous gas was pumped out of the chamber, camp workers—prisoners themselves—pried out the victims' gold teeth and fillings and shaved their hair, which the Germans used to make felt, thread, socks, ropes, and mattresses. Finally, these camp workers disposed of the bodies by burning them in **crematoria** or burying them in mass graves. (As an aside, within a matter of weeks, these camp workers, called *Sonderkommando*, would inevitably meet the same fate as the newly arrived Jews.) With the passage of time, this process became ever more efficient. By the spring of 1944, as many as eight thousand people were gassed each day at Auschwitz-Birkenau.

Prisoners who had avoided both the bullets and the gas might have been considered lucky, but for the misery they would soon endure in the camp. But first, like the corpses in the doomed group, these surviving prisoners had their heads shaved. Then they were forced into showers—actual showers—that were either freezing cold or scalding hot. Next, they exchanged their clothes for a ragged camp uniform—striped pants and a jacket for the men, a smock-type dress for the women, and ill-fitting clogs. On each of these garments was an ID number for the wearer as well as

Holocaust Fact Sheet

- Between 1933, when Hitler came to power, and 1945, when Germany lost World War II, the Nazis murdered more than 11 million people. Approximately 6 million of these were Jews.

- More than 1.1 million children died in the Holocaust.

- Two-thirds of the 9 million European Jews alive in 1933 were killed by the Nazis.

- An estimated 90 percent of all Jews in Poland, Germany, and Austria were killed during the war.

- The most populous ghetto was the Warsaw ghetto. At its peak, more than 400,000 Jews lived there, crammed into an area of just 1.3 square miles (3.4 square kilometers).

- The Einsatzgruppen murdered an estimated 800,000 to 1 million Jews in Soviet territories.

- In September 1941, the Einsatzgruppen killed 34,000 Jews in a period of two days at Babi Yar. This was the deadliest two days for Jews during the Holocaust.

- The first concentration camp, Dachau, opened in 1933.

- By the end of the war, the Nazis had built more than 20,000 camps. Six of these were extermination camps.

- More than 1.1 million people were murdered at Auschwitz-Birkenau—one in six of all Jews killed by the Nazis.

- At Treblinka, another extermination camp, a staff of just 150 people murdered 870,000 Jews.

- Hitler never visited a single concentration camp.

- In May 1943, Germany declared itself *Judenrein* (clean of Jews).

- Approximately 100,000 Jews perished in death marches near the end of the war.

- More than 200,000 people perpetrated the Holocaust.

- Of all the countries occupied by Germany, only one—Albania—had more Jews at the end of the war than it did at the beginning. Albanians, 60 percent of whom were Muslim, provided native Jews and refugees with false papers and hid them when necessary.

- The deadliest year for Jews was 1942. That year, 2.7 million Jews were murdered.

a badge indicating the reason for their imprisonment. For Jews, this badge was typically a yellow star. Finally, workers tattooed an ID number on each prisoner's left forearm.

Human Medical Experimentation

Perhaps the worst fate—worse even than death—was to be made the subject of a human medical experiment. These were performed at several camps, including Auschwitz, Dachau, and Ravensbrück.

The world "cruel" does not begin to describe these experiments. Torture is more apt. Prisoners—many of them children—were subjected to such agonies as having dye injected into their eyes to see if they would change color, experimental surgeries or amputations without anesthesia, being hit on the head repeatedly with a hammer, being immersed in icy water, being left outside without clothes in sub-freezing temperatures for hours at a time and then "rewarmed" in boiling water, being infected with malaria or tuberculosis, being exposed to mustard gas, being forced to drink nothing but seawater, being placed in a pressure chamber, being sterilized, being poisoned, being burned, or being shot, all in the name of "science." If by some miracle a prisoner survived such an experiment, the Nazis typically killed them afterward, dissecting their body and removing their organs for further study.

In one particularly disturbing experiment, Dr. Josef Mengele, who conducted medical experiments at Auschwitz, sewed together a set of twins, "back to back, like Siamese twins." The children's caretaker, a Jewish woman named

Vera Alexander, described the outcome: "Their wounds were infected and oozing pus. They screamed day and night. Then their parents—I remember the mother's name was Stella— managed to get some morphine and they killed the children in order to end their suffering."

Death Marches

In June 1941, the Nazis launched Operation Barbarossa, the code name for its invasion of the Soviet Union—this in spite of the pact that Hitler had made with Stalin prior to the invasion of Poland in 1939. The strategy would prove to be a blunder. Starting in 1944, the Soviets would push the Germans back to their borders—and beyond.

As the Russians pushed the Germans farther and farther west, past the Polish border into German-occupied territory— and, at the same time, the British, French, Canadians, and Americans approached from the west, liberating France, Belgium, and the Netherlands—the Nazis scrambled to hide the evidence of their atrocities. They wanted no survivors to bear witness to their deeds. That meant relocating any surviving inmates in camps outside Germany to camps inside the nation's borders. There, these inmates would continue to serve as forced laborers in support of the war effort. This relocation process commenced in late 1944 and continued until the spring of 1945.

Rather than loading these prisoners onto trains at the camps, camp guards forced prisoners to march to neighboring train depots—sometimes as far as 35 miles (56 km) away— often in bitter cold and with little or no food, water, or rest.

Life in the Camps

Prisoners at German camps who weren't murdered immediately upon arrival faced conditions that were nothing short of brutal. Early each morning, guards awoke the inmates for roll call. This morning roll call often took hours. Prisoners were required to stand completely still in tidy rows until it was over, no matter how long it took, and no matter the weather. During these ordeals (and throughout the rest of the day), prisoners sought to escape the notice of their guards. Part of *Totenkopfverbände* (Death's-Head Detachments), these guards were capriciously cruel. Sometimes, inmates were forced to witness executions. When roll call finally ended, prisoners ate—or, rather, drank—their breakfast, which consisted of imitation coffee or so-called tea.

Next, the prisoners went to work. Some were lucky—they had administrative jobs or worked in the kitchens. Others were less fortunate, relegated to hard labor. Some slaved at factories, coal mines, or quarries. Others dug tunnels or canals or built roads. They worked for hours, although they were permitted a brief break for lunch. This consisted of watery soup with rotten meat and vegetables. Dinner, served at the conclusion of the workday, usually entailed a small piece of black bread and a tiny piece of sausage, some marmalade, or some cheese.

In the evenings, following another interminable roll call, the prisoners returned to their barracks. Women and children shared barracks, while the men were separated into barracks of their own. These windowless structures, built of wood or brick, offered little in the way of comfort. Inmates were crammed

Malnourished prisoners were jammed together and forced to share beds in concentration camps.

three or four to a bunk. There were no mattresses: just wooden planks with straw or rags. Also missing were bathing facilities and a means to wash clothes. For toilets, the prisoners used buckets. Finally, these buildings, which had dirt floors and were often infested with rats and lice, were not insulated. As a result, they were sweltering during the summer and bitter cold during the winter. They did feature stoves, but no fuel was provided.

Escape was nearly impossible. Auschwitz, for example, was surrounded by electrically charged barbed-wire fences. SS guards and dogs patrolled the perimeter. In addition, guards with automatic rifles kept watch from watchtowers. Still, some prisoners made the attempt—although very few succeeded. Those caught attempting escape were summarily executed.

Needless to say, a great many inmates died. Few survived more than a few weeks or months. Some died of disease, some of starvation. Some died of the cold, or from exhaustion or overwork. Some were beaten to death or shot by camp guards. Some were murdered in mass killings. And some, unable to bear the misery, committed suicide.

Any prisoners who fell behind or were unable to continue were immediately shot. Many prisoners died of hypothermia, hunger, or exhaustion along the way. In all, many thousands perished in what came to be called death marches.

Author Elie Wiesel survived one such death march. Later, he wrote about the experience in his famous book, *Night*. "An icy wind blew in violent gusts. But we marched without faltering … Pitch darkness. Every now and then, an explosion in the night. They had orders to fire on any who could not keep up. Their fingers on the triggers, they did not deprive themselves of this pleasure. If one of us had stopped for a second, a sharp shot finished off another filthy son of a bitch." He added, "Near me, men were collapsing in the dirty snow. Shots." (Wiesel, who was awarded a Nobel Peace Prize in 1986 for his decades of work reflecting on the lessons of the Holocaust, passed away in the summer of 2016.)

Jews await selection for the gas chamber or forced labor at Birkenau Station.

Arrival at the train depot offered little relief. Nazi guards crammed the prisoners into open cattle cars, without food, water, or cover. Provided the prisoners survived the days-long journey in these conditions—many did not—they disembarked at their destination, at which point they were again forced to march to their new camp, inside Germany.

Other Victims

Although the Jews were the primary targets of the Nazis, they were not their only victims. The Nazis viewed several other populations as *Untermenschen* (sub-humans). One such population was the Roma people. This group suffered greatly under Nazi rule, facing much the same treatment as the Jews. The Nazis also imprisoned and often killed Jehovah's Witnesses, Freemasons, political opponents, and trade unionists. Slavs in eastern Europe, Soviet prisoners, and Poles were likewise targeted. Indeed, Heinrich Himmler vowed that "All Poles will disappear from the world." Homosexuals— whom the Nazis called "defilers of German blood—also faced imprisonment. Some were castrated or killed.

As for people with mental or physical disabilities, the Nazis sterilized them—at least at first. Later, they simply murdered them outright, usually by gas. To justify these killings, the Nazis claimed the victims were *Lebensunwertes Leben* (life unworthy of life). All these people, the Germans claimed, could not be part of a "racially pure" society.

The Angel of Death

Josef Mengele was born in March 1911 in Bavaria. A strong student, Mengele studied medicine at Goethe University Frankfurt and philosophy and anthropology at the University of Munich.

In 1937, Mengele joined the Nazi Party and, later, the SS. After the start of World War II, Mengele volunteered for medical service, eventually landing at Auschwitz. There, he was appointed chief physician.

At Auschwitz, Mengele performed horrific medical experiments on live human subjects, usually children. At first, the children on whom Mengele performed his experiments were treated well. They were given better food, enjoyed more comfortable living conditions, and had access to a playground. Often, Mengele—who introduced himself to these children as "Onkel (Uncle) Mengele"— gave them sweets. But when it came to work, Mengele—known

Dr. Joseph Mengele, the "Angel of Death," performed horrific medical experiments on prisoners—usually children.

as the "Angel of Death"—personally tortured these children without remorse.

As observed by a former Auschwitz prisoner doctor in the book *The Nazi Doctors: Medical Killing and the Psychology of Genocide*, "[Mengele] was capable of being so kind to the children, to have them become fond of him, to bring them sugar, to think of small details in their daily lives, and to do things we would genuinely admire." The witness continued, "And then, next to that ... the crematoria smoke, and these children, tomorrow or in a half-hour, he is going to send them there. Well, that is where the anomaly lay."

Mengele was never called to account for his crimes. After the war, he escaped to South America, where he died a free man in 1979.

Major Perpetrators

Who was to blame for all these atrocities? Of course, primary responsibility must fall on the shoulders of Adolf Hitler. It was Hitler who served as head of the Nazi Party and who directed its actions. But Hitler did not act alone. Members of his inner circle were key in the implementation of Hitler's plans.

One was Hermann Göring, who had been a member of the Nazi Party for nearly as long as Hitler had. During Hitler's rule, Göring served as the commander in chief of the German Luftwaffe (air force). Later, Hitler named Göring as his successor and deputy of all his offices (although Hitler would later change his mind). For much of the war, Göring occupied himself with acquiring property and art, much of it stolen from Jewish victims of the Holocaust. He was also responsible for the formation of the Gestapo.

Soon after Göring formed the Gestapo, he surrendered command of that organization to Heinrich Himmler, who would become among the most powerful men in Germany. In addition to overseeing the Gestapo and other police and security forces), Himmler established and controlled the extensive network of Nazi camps, including extermination camps.

Joseph Goebbels served as the head of the Reich Ministry for Popular Entertainment and Propaganda. Goebbels controlled the flow of all information in Germany and was instrumental in turning the German public against the Jews. Immediately before his death, Hitler would cast Göring aside and name Goebbels as his successor.

Another key figure was Adolf Eichmann. His job was to organize the deportation of Jews to ghettos and camps in eastern Europe. He did so without remorse. In the classic book *The Rise and Fall of the Third Reich: A History of Nazi Germany*, Eichmann is reported to have said toward the end of the war that "he would leap laughing into the grave because the feeling that he had five million people on his conscience would be for him a source of extraordinary satisfaction."

Reinhard Heydrich—described by Hitler himself as "the man with the iron heart"—also played a significant role in the crimes against the Jews. Heydrich was a key organizer behind Kristallnacht and the driving force in the formation of the Einsatzgruppen. It was Heydrich who called the Wannsee Conference, which outlined the so-called Final Solution.

But no action as far sweeping as the Holocaust could have been perpetrated by just these few people. Every office in the German government played its part. The Interior Ministry identified those Germans who were Jews. The post office distributed orders for the denaturalization and deportation of German Jews. The Finance Ministry seized Jewish assets. Government-run trains carried Jews to the camps. German police forces and camp guards tortured and killed Jews. The list goes on and on.

It wasn't just the government, however. German businesses of all sizes and types played their part. They fired Jewish workers. They marginalized Jewish stockholders. Dehomag, the German arm of IBM, used punch-card machines to compile comprehensive lists of victims. The German National Bank helped launder valuables stolen from the Jews. German construction companies built camps. German pharmaceutical companies used camp inmates to test drugs. In addition, several German companies used inmates imprisoned at forced-labor camps as free labor—and grew very rich as a result. These included IG Farben, ThyssenKrupp, BMW, Daimler (Mercedes), Bosch, Audi, and VW.

And of course, there were the individual Germans— private citizens of the Reich and the territory it occupied. Some individuals attempted to help the Jews, often at great personal cost. But far more viewed the plight of the Jews as insignificant or, worse, actively aided in the Nazis' efforts to dehumanize and destroy the Jews. In all, experts estimate that more than two hundred thousand people played a direct role in the perpetration of the Holocaust.

FOUR

Defiance

Initially, the Jews did not recognize the danger in which they found themselves. After all, the Germans did not reveal their plans for the Jews all at once. Rather, their murderous aims became evident over a period of many years. By the time the Jews understood their predicament, it was too late to organize widespread resistance.

There was another reason the Jews were slow to react. According to author Paul Johnson in his *A History of the Jews*, "The Jews had been persecuted for a millennium and a half and had learned from long experience that resistance cost lives rather than saved them. Their history, their theology, their folklore, their social structure, even their vocabulary trained them to negotiate, to pay, to plead, to protest, not to fight."

Holocaust survivor Alexander Kimel concurred. "I believe that although there were many factors that inhibited our responses, the most important factors were isolation and historical conditioning to accepting martyrdom."

Opposite: Jewish insurgents fight in the streets of Warsaw during the Warsaw Ghetto Uprising, which ended with the burning of the ghetto.

In time, that would change. Jews found ways to resist their oppressors. Sometimes that meant engaging in passive resistance. Historian Martin Gilbert explained:

> In every ghetto, in every deportation train, in every labor camp, even in the death camps, the will to resist was strong, and took many forms. Fighting with the few weapons that would be found, individual acts of defiance and protest, the courage of obtaining food and water under the threat of death, the superiority of refusing to allow the Germans their final wish to gloat over panic and despair. Even passivity was a form of resistance. To die with dignity was a form of resistance. To resist the demoralizing, brutalizing force of evil, to refuse to be reduced to the level of animals, to live through the torment, to outlive the tormentors, these too were acts of resistance.

Among the Jews, even mere survival came to be considered an act of resistance. But the Jews did not engage only in passive resistance. As the war wore on, they performed more overt acts of defiance. They formed resistance groups in Germany and abroad. Some of these were even armed. Jews in ghettos and concentration camps rose up. As observed by Pieter Meerburg, a Christian whose work in the Dutch Resistance saved many Jewish children, "Many people think the Jews went to their deaths like sheep to the slaughter, and that's not true—it's absolutely not true. I worked closely with many Jewish people in the Resistance, and I can tell you, they took much greater risks than I did."

Jewish Resistance in Germany

Some Jews in Germany resisted Nazi rule. One way to do this was to engage in sabotage. Another was to funnel intelligence to Allied forces. Yet another was to issue anti-Nazi propaganda. Jews also forged documents and identity cards to help others escape.

Although much of this resistance activity occurred on an individual basis, there were a few Jewish resistance groups in Germany. Perhaps the most significant of these was the Baum Gruppe (Baum Group). Based in Berlin, this group, which consisted primarily of younger Jews, was active from 1937 to 1942. In addition to handing out anti-Nazi propaganda and organizing demonstrations, the Baum Gruppe bombed an anti-Soviet exhibition in Berlin. Groups who advocated the creation of a Jewish state in Palestine, called **Zionist** groups, also engaged in resistance efforts.

Armed Jewish Resistance

Starting in 1938, Jews in Germany were banned from owning weapons of any kind, including firearms and even knives. As a result, Jewish resistance groups in Germany were generally unarmed. Outside Germany, however—in eastern Europe, in France, in the Netherlands, in Italy, and elsewhere—some Jews took up arms against the Germans and their collaborators. These Jews engaged in guerrilla warfare, sabotaged German operations, incited ghetto uprisings, freed prisoners, killed German soldiers, and assassinated collaborators.

Often, these Jews were part of larger resistance movements. An estimated thirty thousand Jews joined with Soviet **partisans** against the Nazis. Jews were also active in the Dutch Resistance and the French Resistance. Alternatively, Jews formed smaller groups of their own. Perhaps the most famous of these was the Bielski partisans, named after four brothers who founded the group: Tuvia, Alexander (Zus), Asael, and Aron Bielski. The Bielski brothers came from a family of millers and farmers near Novogrodek, in Poland. In 1939, Soviet troops occupied Novogrodek. Two years later, in 1941, Germans overran the town. Nazi officials forced all Jews in Novogrodek and surrounding towns into a ghetto, including the Bielski family.

In August 1941, Nazis murdered the Bielski brothers' parents and siblings. The brothers, however, escaped to the nearby Naliboki Forest. Soon, they and several other partisan fighters began resistance operations. They ambushed German soldiers and collaborators, killing them and claiming their

Many Jews, including women, joined partisan militia groups.

weapons for their own use; they blew up bridges; and they derailed trains carrying German troops and supplies.

In time, the group's numbers grew. At its peak, the group boasted more than 1,200 members—all Jews. No one was turned away. Indeed, women, children, and the elderly comprised nearly 70 percent of the group's numbers. The group's leader, Tuvia Bielski, believed "To save a Jew is much more important than to kill Germans."

At first, the group moved from place to place to evade capture. Eventually, members built a camp deep in the forest. This camp featured underground dugouts, used for housing. It also included several semipermanent structures, such as a metal shop, to repair damaged weapons and build new ones; a tannery, to produce the leather needed to make shoes, belts, bridles, and saddles; a mill, a bakery, and a kitchen, to feed the partisans (several cows supplied milk); a bathhouse; a medical clinic for the wounded and a quarantine hut for the sick; a school; and a synagogue. There was even a court of law and a jail.

Not all group members engaged in resistance activities. Indeed, most stayed behind to sustain camp operations. Some cooked. Some tended to the children. Some patched up old clothing and shoes, or made new ones. Residents who had been carpenters, hatmakers, watchmakers, barbers— whatever their trade—offered their services to the group as needed.

The Bielski partisans were so disruptive, so effective, that the Nazis offered a handsome reward for the capture of their leader, Tuvia. But they never caught him—or any of his brothers.

Jews in unoccupied countries took up arms as members of Allied military forces. One group, called the Jewish Brigade, comprised of thousands of Jewish volunteers from the British Mandate of Palestine, fought as part of the larger British Army. Members of this brigade parachuted into Europe to organize resistance efforts. Among these was twenty-three-year-old Hannah Senesh, dropped behind German lines in June 1944 to help rescue Hungarian Jews bound for Auschwitz. Unfortunately, Senesh was captured. Nazi operatives imprisoned and tortured her, but she did not betray her mission. Ultimately, they executed her by firing squad.

Resistance in Jewish Ghettos

Resistance was not limited to those Jews who roamed free. Jews held captive in ghettos also rose up—sometimes with arms. This was the case during the Warsaw Ghetto Uprising.

What prompted this rebellion? Starting in 1942, the Nazis began mass deportations of Jews in the ghetto. They told the Jews they would be "resettled" in labor camps. In fact, these Jews—as many as three hundred thousand in all—were taken to the Treblinka extermination camps and gassed.

Eventually, word of this crime reached those Jews still in the ghetto. In response, many of the remaining inhabitants—mostly young Jews—vowed to resist. They formed an organization called the *Zydowska Organizacja Bojowa* (Jewish Combat Organization), or ZOB. Soon, the group expanded to incorporate members of other underground organizations and made contact with the larger Polish Resistance, who provided training, arms, and even explosives.

The ZOB, led by twenty-three-year-old Mordecai Anielewicz, urged all Jews in the ghetto to fight back when the Germans attempted to pack them into the railroad cars bound for Treblinka. In January 1943, ghetto residents did just that. As German troops tried to round up the next group for deportation, large numbers of residents took to the streets. The ploy worked. Thousands of Jews were spared deportation.

Emboldened, the ZOB planned a full-scale rebellion. They built underground bunkers, where women, children, and the elderly could hide. They dug tunnels and constructed passageways to ensure freedom of movement. They smuggled in handguns and grenades. Thanks to sympathetic groups outside the ghetto, like the *Zydowski Zwiazek Wojskowy* (Jewish Military Union), they even got their hands on three rifles, two land mines, and a submachine gun. They executed known Nazi collaborators within the ghetto. When German troops again entered the ghetto to round up the remaining inhabitants in April 1943, the Jews fought back.

Did the Jews in the Warsaw ghetto believe they would beat back the Germans? No. They knew they were doomed. But it was important to them to die with honor, on their own terms. Yitzhak Zuckerman, who assisted the insurrection from the outside and lived to tell the tale, recalled, "This was a war of less than a thousand people against a mighty army and no one doubted how it was likely to turn out … The really important things were inherent in the force shown by Jewish youths, after years of degradation, to rise up against their destroyers, and determine what death they would choose: Treblinka or Uprising."

German soldiers set fire to the Warsaw ghetto to flush out the rebels.

Still, these courageous fighters held German forces at bay for nearly a month. They lost only when the Germans set fire to the ghetto, building by building, flushing the rebels out. "We were beaten by the flames, not the Germans," recalled Marek Edelman, a leader of the uprising and one of the few survivors, in a newspaper story. (He escaped through a sewer.) Thousands of Jews were killed in the clash. Except for the few Jews who managed to escape, all who survived the uprising were deported to extermination camps and murdered.

Resistance in Camps

There are several accounts of escape attempts from German camps. In one attempt, in early 1942, a lone inmate escaped from the Chełmno extermination camp. In another attempt, this one in June 1942, four male inmates at Auschwitz escaped the camp by posing as SS officers, stealing a camp vehicle, and simply driving out. They were never caught. These and other escape attempts served as inspiration to prisoners still inside the camps. But sometimes, they served an even greater purpose: they enabled escapees to report camp atrocities to Jews on the outside and to the world at large (although at first, no one believed them).

Not all escapes were successful. Indeed, most were not. Nor were the three major uprisings that occurred at various extermination camps toward the end of the war. The first of these occurred in August 1943, at Treblinka. Inmates stole guns and grenades from the camp armory and used them to attack Nazi guards. Prisoners also disabled military vehicles and set fire to barracks and warehouses. To quell the uprising, camp guards opened fire, killing approximately 1,500 prisoners. In the chaos, some 300 inmates attempted escape. Most were slaughtered by Germans in pursuit.

The second was in October 1943, at Sobibór. Prisoners there concocted a plan to kill all the camp guards and simply walk out the front gate. Unfortunately, they fell short of their objective—although they did manage to shoot eleven SS officers and several camp guards before facing heavy fire. Several hundred prisoners made a break for freedom, but again, most were killed.

Captain Witold Pilecki

Most people wanted *out* of the camps. One man, Captain Witold Pilecki of the Polish Cavalry, a member of the Polish underground, wanted *in*. His plan was to gather intelligence and organize an insurrection inside Auschwitz.

In September 1940, Pilecki snuck into the camp. While there, he successfully sparked a resistance movement and managed to funnel intelligence to Allied forces. In 1943, his mission complete, he escaped the camp.

Pilecki survived the war. However, he was executed in May 1948 by Communist authorities in Poland, who accused him of spying for the Polish government in exile.

The third major uprising occurred in Auschwitz-Birkenau in October 1944. Using explosives smuggled into the camp, some 250 Sonderkommandos (inmates who were forced to burn the corpses of prisoners killed in the gas chambers) blew up one of the crematoria. Afterward, they, too, attempted escape, but nearly all were slain.

Outside Help

During the Holocaust, Europeans who were *not* Jewish reacted in one of four ways: by becoming bystanders, perpetrators, collaborators, or rescuers. Bystanders were the most common. They believed that what was happening to the Jews was none of their business or were too terrified to intervene. Also common were the perpetrators and collaborators. These people personally inflicted abuse on the Jews or cooperated with the Nazis to do so. A very small minority became rescuers. These rescuers helped the Jews—and at great personal risk. How did they help? Sometimes, the rescuers provided shelter for Jews for a brief period or hid them for an extended duration. Other times, the rescuers helped Jews cross into neighboring countries. Or, they supplied papers, food, clothing, money, and even weapons.

People who helped the Jews did so at great personal risk. If caught by the Nazis, they were subject to arrest, imprisonment, interrogation, torture, deportation, or execution.

Nazi interrogation and torture techniques were merciless. Prisoners were brutally beaten—sometimes even to death. Often, prisoners were denied food and water or kept awake for days on end. Prisoners condemned to death might die by hanging. Or they might be shot. Some were beheaded. Some were strangled and hung from a meat hook.

The Nazis didn't only punish those who sheltered Jews, however. Often, they punished that person's entire family. This may partially explain why few people subject to Nazi rule attempted to help the Jews.

Still, there are countless stories of private individuals who did help the Jews. Perhaps the most famous of these is the story of Oskar Schindler, depicted in the 1993 film *Schindler's List*. Schindler saved the lives of more than 1,200 Jews by claiming they were indispensable to his company. A Dutch industrialist named Frits Philips saved nearly 400 Jews in a

Who Was Anne Frank?

When the Nazis came to power, the Frank family, who were Jewish, sought safety in Amsterdam, the Netherlands. Anne's father, Otto, started his own business there. For a time, the family was out of danger. But in 1940, the Germans conquered the Netherlands. Once again, the Frank family was living under Nazi control. In July 1942, Anne's family went into hiding on an upper floor of Otto's business. His staff helped them to survive.

During their years in hiding, Anne kept a diary. She wrote about her family and about life in hiding. She wrote about her feelings and her fears. Sadly, there are no entries in the diary after August 4, 1944. That's when Nazis raided the Frank family's hiding place and sent them to Auschwitz. Anne's mother, Edith, died soon thereafter. In October, Anne and her sister Margot were transferred to Bergen-Belsen. In March 1945, both girls died of typhus. Anne was just fifteen years old.

Otto Frank survived the war. When he found Anne's diary, he published it in 1947 under the title *Anne Frank: The Diary of a Young Girl*. It remains one of the most touching and resonant accounts of life during the Holocaust.

Anne Frank kept a record of her days in hiding. Her diary was published by her father after the war.

similar manner. It wasn't just wealthy factory owners who helped the Jews, however. A sewage inspector named Leopold Socha sheltered Jews in the sewers in the Polish city of Lwów. The director of the Warsaw zoo, Jan Zabinski, concealed Jews on zoo property. And a Dutch woman named Miep Gies helped to hide Anne Frank and her family inside her place of work.

Sometimes, whole villages conspired to shelter Jews. One was Le Chambon-sur-Lignon, in France. Led by a local priest, the inhabitants of this village hid Jews in private homes, local farms, public buildings, and, when Nazi patrols approached the village, in the surrounding countryside. Villagers in Le Chambon-sur-Lignon also helped Jews cross the border to safety in nearby Switzerland.

Incredibly, even some German officers attempted to help the Jews, putting themselves in great peril. One officer in the Wehrmacht, Major Karl Plagge, issued almost one thousand work permits to Jews in an effort to save them. Another, Albert Battel, blocked SS officers from deporting residents of the Jewish ghetto in Poland where he was stationed. Yet another, Wilm Hosenfeld, hid several Jews in occupied Poland, including a famous composer named Władysław Szpilman. (Szpilman's story is depicted in the movie *The Pianist*.)

Starting in 1963, the Holocaust memorial in Israel, Yad Vashem, began recognizing non-Jews who risked their lives to save Jews from the Nazis. Thus far, Yad Vesham has recognized more than twenty-four thousand such people from forty-four countries around the world, calling them Righteous Among the Nations.

FIVE

The Fallout

In her diary, Anne Frank wrote, "In spite of everything, I still believe that people are really good at heart. I simply can't build up my hopes on a foundation consisting of confusion, misery, and death. I see the world gradually being turned into a wilderness, I hear the ever approaching thunder, which will destroy us too, I can feel the sufferings of millions and yet, if I look up into the heavens, I think that it will all come right, that this cruelty too will end, and that peace and tranquility will return again." Anne Frank was right. The thunder would destroy her, and most of her family, too. But eventually, as Anne predicted, the cruelty inflicted by the Nazis did end.

The Defeat of Hitler

For a time, it seemed as though the Nazis were unstoppable. In a span of just two years—1940 and 1941—the Germans conquered Denmark, Norway, Belgium, the Netherlands, Luxembourg, France, Yugoslavia, and Greece. They also attacked Great Britain by air and invaded the USSR.

Opposite: Londoners pile onto a bus to celebrate the end of World War II in Europe on V-E Day..

This last action, code-named Operation Barbarossa, would prove Hitler's undoing. During the winter of 1942–1943, the Soviet army, often called the Red Army, surrounded the Germans at Stalingrad, forcing them to surrender. In time, Soviet troops pushed the German army all the way back to the Soviet border—and in April 1945, into Germany itself.

As the Soviets pushed westward toward Germany, American, British, Canadian, and Free French troops pushed east. On June 6, 1944, this coalition of Western Allies stormed the beaches of Normandy, France, then under German control. This event—originally referred to as Operation Overlord and now called D-Day—gave them a much-needed foothold on the European continent. From this foothold, the Western Allies marched on to liberate all of France, as well as Belgium and the Netherlands, from the Nazis. And in March 1945, coalition forces crossed the Rhine into Germany. (Interestingly, one reason German forces were unable to fend off their enemies on both fronts was that they had tied up too many resources in their efforts to exterminate the Jews.)

For much of this time, Hitler—who had by then retreated to an underground bunker in Berlin called the *Führerbunker*—remained in denial about the state of the war. He appeared to believe that the Germans would repel these Allied advances. In April 1945, Hitler ordered a desperation attack on Russian troops by a German army detachment that was both undermanned and underequipped. The next day, his commanders informed him that the attack hadn't just failed—it had never taken place. Worse, the Soviet army had

The Denazification of Germany

Following Germany's collapse, the Allies issued a series of directives aimed at the **denazification** of Germany. In other words, they sought to rid German society, culture, and government of all vestiges of Nazism, including physical symbols such as swastikas. One way they achieved this was by destroying any monuments, statues, or signs connected to Nazism. Another was to remove all Nazi propaganda—including anti-Jewish propaganda—from German life. Allied officials also attempted to identify and punish all members of the Nazi Party, but this effort was less successful.

entered Berlin. At last, Hitler understood he was defeated. Enraged, Hitler accused his commanders of incompetence and treachery. He then declared that "everything was lost." Still, he said, he would remain in Berlin until the bitter end.

Hitler may have given up hope, but his associates had not. Goebbels urged the citizens of Berlin to repel the Red Army. This proved futile. Göring attempted to wrest control of the German government from Hitler. In response, Hitler had Göring arrested and removed him from all government positions. Himmler, without Hitler's knowledge, contacted Allied leaders to discuss terms of surrender. He, too, was arrested, and his assistant was shot.

On April 30, as the Red Army closed in on the center of Berlin, Hitler—no doubt aware of what painful fate awaited him in the event he was captured—committed suicide. Goebbels assumed the role of chancellor, while Grand Admiral Karl Dönitz took over as head of state.

Goebbels's chancellorship would be short-lived, however. On May 1, Goebbels and his wife, Magda, committed suicide—after killing all six of their young children with cyanide. That left Dönitz as the sole leader of the German government.

With Hitler gone and the Nazi leadership in shambles, and with Allied forces pressing in on all sides, it was merely a matter of days before Germany surrendered unconditionally. It did so on May 8, 1945, now referred to as Victory in Europe Day, or more commonly, V-E Day.

Liberation

As Allied forces closed in on Germany, they discovered the camps that the Nazis had used to imprison and exterminate Jews. Upon their arrival at each camp, these Allied troops liberated what prisoners remained.

The first of these was Majdanek, liberated by the Soviets in July 1944. The Soviets also liberated Chełmno and Auschwitz, both in January 1945; Ravensbrück (April 1945); and Theresienstadt (May 1945). Unites States forces liberated Buchenwald and Dachau in April 1945. That same month, the British liberated Bergen-Belsen. Three camps were never liberated, however: Treblinka, Sobibór, and Bełzec. These were destroyed by the Nazis before the Allies arrived.

What the liberators found was sickening. Richard Dimbleby of the British Broadcasting Corporation (BBC) described the scene at Bergen-Belsen: "Here over an acre of ground lay dead and dying people. You could not see which was which. The living lay with their heads against the corpses and around them moved the awful, ghostly procession of emaciated, aimless people, with nothing to do and with no hope of life, unable to move out of your way, unable to look at the terrible sights around them." Corpses, said one American soldier, had been "stacked up like cordwood." As General Dwight D. Eisenhower, among the first Americans to see Buchenwald, wrote to his wife, "I never dreamed that such cruelty, bestiality, and savagery could really exist in this world."

Young prisoners at Dachau greet their American liberators.

Holocaust Deniers

To document German atrocities, Allied forces filmed these camps and the survivors they found there. This footage was then broadcast in cinemas all over the world, shocking all who saw it.

Incredibly, despite this footage, and despite accounts of thousands of survivors, there are those who deny the Holocaust ever took place. These so-called Holocaust deniers—part of an anti-Semitic movement that continues to this day—believe the Holocaust is a hoax, perpetrated by the Jews to advance their own interests, despite overwhelming evidence to the contrary. In Germany, it is illegal to deny the Holocaust.

The Survivors

There are many tragic stories about World War II. Perhaps the most tragic is that some fourteen thousand Jews who had lived to see liberation died within their first week of freedom, despite efforts by Allied troops, aid organizations, and fellow prisoners to treat them. Some were simply too far gone—from disease, from starvation, from exhaustion—by the time Allied forces arrived, to rally. Others couldn't digest the first morsels of "proper" food they'd consumed in years and died as a result.

Those who survived faced a nearly insurmountable task: rebuilding their lives. Foremost on all their minds was tracking down lost relatives—assuming they had survived. This proved an exercise in frustration, as there was no coordinated effort to achieve this. As noted by Earl G. Harrison, an American attorney dispatched by President Harry S. Truman to survey the camps, "The most absorbing worry of these Nazi and war victims concerns relatives—wives, husbands, parents, children. Most of them have been separated for three, four or five years and they cannot understand why the liberators should not have undertaken immediately the organized effort to reunite family groups."

Beyond that, they had to determine where they would go. This was no small matter given that the Nazis had stripped them of their homes—not to mention all their money, possessions, and in some cases even their citizenship—during the war. Initially, efforts were made to repatriate Jews to their country of origin. Often, however, these Jews faced opposition from the non-Jews in the area. Typically, this was because these non-Jews had assumed ownership of the homes and belongings of Jews who had been deported during the war and were loath to return them. Sometimes, they resorted to violence to maintain the status quo. On July 4, 1946, anti-Semites murdered forty-two Holocaust survivors in the Polish town of Kielce.

It soon became clear that for many Jews, returning to their place of origin simply was not possible. These Jews chose to emigrate. The vast majority sought admittance to Palestine, although some would settle for other countries like the United States. As before, however, these countries limited the number of immigrants allowed in. Until these restrictions were eased, these Jews had no choice but to wait in one of various displaced persons (DP) camps across Europe. At their zenith, these camps housed as many as 250,000 displaced Jews.

These camps were little better than the concentration camps of old. Indeed, many of these camps *were* concentration camps—or they had been until the end of the war. Yes, prisoners weren't starved, beaten, or worked to death. Still, they found themselves, to quote Harrison, "living under guard behind barbed-wire fences ... amidst crowded, frequently unsanitary and generally grim conditions."

Families arrive at a displaced persons (DP) camp in Germany.

"Many of the Jewish displaced persons ... had no clothing other than their concentration camp garb ... while others, to their chagrin, were obliged to wear German SS uniforms," Harrison continued. "As matters now stand, we appear to be treating the Jews as the Nazis treated them except that we do not exterminate them. They are in concentration camps in large numbers under our military guard instead of SS troops."

Formation of a Jewish State

The events of the Holocaust and the number of displaced Jews fueled the desire for a Jewish homeland in the Middle East. For these Jews, the natural choice was Palestine. After all, they reasoned, it was their ancestral homeland. And besides, some sixty thousand Jews had already sought refuge there in the years before the war. There was just one problem: the British, who governed the region, continued to restrict immigration in an effort to keep peace with local Arabs.

Desperate to leave Europe, many Jews simply disregarded this policy. They organized an underground effort, called Bricha, to smuggle Holocaust survivors to Italy, onto ships, and through the British cordon into Palestine. Many Jews crossed into Palestine safely. But others were caught en route. Those who were caught were sent to detention camps on the island of Cyprus (also controlled by the British) or to DP camps in Europe.

It was not lost on the international community that the Jews had been liberated from concentration camps only to find themselves imprisoned once again, either in displacement camps or in detention camps. In January 1946, President

Truman pressured the British government to ease immigration restrictions in Palestine. The British government, in turn, referred the issue to the United Nations. (Formed after the war, the United Nations—which replaced the League of Nations—is an intergovernmental organization dedicated to the promotion of international cooperation.)

In November 1947, the United Nations put the matter to a vote. The result: British Palestine would be split into two new states. One of these states, called Palestine, would be an Arab state. The other, called Israel, would belong to the Jews. In early 1948, the British commenced their withdrawal from the area, and on May 14 of that same year, the state of Israel was officially born. David Ben-Gurion, the first prime minister of Israel, announced open immigration to all Jews. This, he said, "would solve the problem of Jewish homelessness by opening the gates to all Jews and lifting the Jewish people to equality in the family of nations." Between 1948 and 1951, some seven hundred thousand Jews would move to Israel—including more than two-thirds of the displaced persons in Europe. Soon thereafter, the United States eased its immigration restrictions.

The Nuremberg Trials

What became of the Nazis who perpetrated the Holocaust? Hitler and Goebbels committed suicide, but what of Heydrich, Himmler, Göring, Eichmann, and other top Nazi officials responsible for the deaths of millions of Jews?

Heydrich—the "man with an iron heart"—was assassinated in June 1942 in Prague, Czechoslovakia, by a team of Czech

German Reparations ... Again

Following World War II, the Germans were subject to reparations, just as they had been after World War I. This time, however, the reparations—amounting to $845 million—were paid to Israel to help cover the cost of the hundreds of thousands of Jews who emigrated there, and to individual Jews who had been harmed by the Nazis. West Germany paid an additional $125 million in reparations to Israel in 1988. And in 1999, to avoid lawsuits against German businesses such as Deutsche Bank, Siemens, and BMW, which had profited from Jewish slave laborers during the war, the German government raised $5 billion to distribute to any slave laborers still alive.

and Slovak soldiers trained by the British. Himmler committed suicide in May 1945 to avoid capture by the Soviets. As for Göring, he was taken into custody by American forces, also in May 1945. Starting in November of that year, Göring and twenty-three other high-ranking Nazis were put on trial by the International Military Tribunal (IMT), comprising judges from the United States, Great Britain, France, and the Soviet Union. These trials, which took place in November 1945 in Nuremberg, Germany, were called the Nuremberg trials. (These men were just some of the Nazis put on trial during the Nuremberg trials. In all, some two hundred Nazis were tried at Nuremberg.)

The charges: participation in a common plan or conspiracy for the accomplishment of a crime against peace; planning, initiating and waging wars of aggression and other crimes against peace; war crimes; and crimes against humanity—"namely, murder, extermination, enslavement, deportation, and other inhumane acts committed against any civilian population, before or during the war; or persecution on political, racial, or religious grounds in execution of or in connection with any crime within the jurisdiction of the Tribunal, whether or not in violation of domestic law of the country where perpetrated."

The Nuremberg trials were held to prosecute Nazis for war crimes. Hermann Göring is seated with his elbow on the railing. Göring was sentenced to death.

Revenge

Some Jews, including several Jewish partisans who had resisted the Nazis, did not wait for justice to take its course. They sought revenge. One group of these Jews, called the Nokmim (Hebrew for "avengers"), killed several former Nazis. Some they hanged. Others they strangled. Still others they killed in hit-and-run attacks. In one famous case, the Nokmim attempted to poison several former SS members who were inmates at Stalag 13, a prisoner-of-war camp in Nuremberg, by adding arsenic to their bread rations. This attempt failed, however.

Twelve of these high-ranking officials, including Göring, were sentenced to death by hanging—although Göring would commit suicide the day before his scheduled execution. Seven received prison sentences—three for life, and four ranging from ten to twenty years—at Spandau Prison in Berlin. Three were acquitted.

After the war, Eichmann escaped to Argentina. Eventually, a Holocaust survivor–turned–Nazi hunter named Simon Wiesenthal located Eichmann, after which Israeli intelligence agents kidnapped him and brought him to Jerusalem. There, Eichmann was tried by an Israeli court for crimes against the Jewish people, crimes against humanity, and more. The court found Eichmann guilty and sentenced him to death by hanging—the first and only time an Israeli court has issued a death sentence. He was executed in 1962.

Continued Conflict

One would think that after the Holocaust, the citizens of the world might decide never to engage in genocide again. Sadly, that has not been the case. Since the Holocaust, there have been several genocides all over the globe.

From 1975 to 1979, under the leadership of Pol Pot, the Communist Party in Cambodia, called the Khmer Rouge, murdered an estimated 1.7 million Cambodians. From 1992 to 1995,

Nazi hunter Serge Klarsfeld and his wife, Beate, received Legion of Honor medals.

Serbs in Bosnia sought to "cleanse" the country of Bosnian Muslims, called Bosniaks. Some eighty thousand Bosniaks were killed, including some eight thousand boys and men from the town of Srebrenica. In 1994, a Rwandan tribe called the Hutus slaughtered anywhere from five hundred thousand to one million members of another tribe called the Tutsis—as much as 70 percent of the total Tutsi population. This occurred over the course of just one hundred days. These are just a few examples of more recent incidences of genocide.

While the Jews have not been subject to another genocide, their persecution continues. A US State Department report issued in March 2008 reported an increase in anti-Semitism all over the world. This finding was supported by another report, released in 2012, by the US Bureau of Democracy, Human Rights, and Labor.

One hotspot that remains is in the Middle East. This is in large part due to the Israeli-Palestinian conflict, which began when the United Nations divided Palestine into two states—Israel for the Jews, and Palestine for the Arabs—in 1948. While the Jews were thrilled with the UN's decision, the Palestinians—who themselves sought autonomy over all of British Palestine—were not. As a result, Israel found itself under attack by Arab forces almost immediately after attaining statehood. In this first conflict, Israel prevailed. It not only retained the area it had been given by the UN, it also claimed almost 60 percent of the land assigned to the Arab Palestinians. The remaining Palestinian land was divided between Egypt and Jordan. The Palestinians were displaced from their homes and left without a country.

Israel spent the next twenty years under near constant attack. Tensions heightened further in 1967. That year, after attacks by various Arab forces, Israel seized control of the Gaza Strip and Sinai Peninsula from Egypt, of East Jerusalem and the West Bank from Jordan, and the Golan Heights from Syria during a conflict that is now called the Six-Day War. Since that time, Israel has retained possession of most of this land. Some cities, such as Bethlehem, have been returned to Palestinian control. There have been many acts of violence carried out by both Muslims and Jews, some provoked by the building of unauthorized Jewish settlements on Palestinian land.

Although there have been many attempts to broker peace between Israel and the Palestinians who remain in their original territory and the Arab world in general—perhaps by reinstating the State of Palestine—these efforts have thus far proved unsuccessful. This has led many to describe the Israeli-Palestinian conflict as the world's "most intractable conflict." Dehumanization of the Jews continues with the broadcast of blood libel propaganda stories on Arab TV shows and websites.

Never Again

It is incumbent upon all people to ensure that an event as sweeping and deadly as the Holocaust never happens again. That requires vigilance and the courage to stand up against those who would perpetrate such a crime. In the famous words of Martin Niemöller, who bravely spoke out against

Lutheran Pastor Martin Niemöller spoke out against the Nazis and was sent to a concentration camp as punishment; here he protests against the Vietnam War in 1968.

the Nazis and spent seven years in concentration camps as a result:

> First they came for the socialists, and I did not speak out—because I was not a socialist.
>
> Then they came for the trade unionists, and I did not speak out—because I was not a trade unionist.
>
> Then they came for the Jews, and I did not speak out—because I was not a Jew.
>
> Then they came for me—and there was no one left to speak for me.

Major Events of the Nazi Persecution

April 20, 1889: Adolf Hitler is born.

June 28, 1914: Archduke Franz Ferdinand of Austria and his wife are assassinated.

July 28, 1914: The Great War, also known as World War I, begins.

November 11, 1918: The Great War ends with the surrender of Germany.

June 28, 1919: Germany signs the Treaty of Versailles.

July 1921: Hitler assumes control of the Nazi Party.

November 8–9, 1923: Hitler and his henchmen attempt a coup in Munich, called the Beer Hall Putsch. The coup is a failure and Hitler is sent to prison, where he writes *Mein Kampf*.

December 19, 1924: Hitler is released from prison.

July 31, 1932: The Nazi Party becomes the largest party in the German Reichstag.

January 30, 1933: Hitler is appointed chancellor of Germany.

March 23, 1933: The Reichstag passes the Enabling Act, giving Hitler absolute power.

April 1, 1933: Nazis organize a boycott of Jewish businesses.

April 7, 1933: The Nazis pass the Law for the Restoration of the Professional Civil Service, the first of many anti-Semitic laws.

May 10, 1933: Nazis burn thousands of books associated with an "un-German spirit."

September 15, 1935: The Nazis pass the Nuremberg Laws.

March 12, 1938: The Nazis annex Austria, an event called the *Anschluss*.

October 10, 1938: The Nazis annex the Sudetenland, part of Czechoslovakia. Soon, they conquer the entire country.

November 9–10, 1938: Nazis incite riots all over Germany, resulting in the destruction of Jewish homes, businesses, and synagogues, and the arrest of some thirty thousand Jews. This event is now known as Kristallnacht, or "Night of Broken Glass."

November 15, 1938: Jewish children are expelled from German public schools.

September 1, 1939: Germany invades Poland, starting World War II.

June 22, 1941: The Germans launch Operation Barbarossa, the code name for their invasion of the Soviet Union.

September 3, 1941: Zyklon-B gas is first used to murder prisoners at Auschwitz.

September 28–30, 1941: Some thirty-four thousand Soviet Jews are massacred by *Einsatzgruppen* and buried in a mass grave at Babi Yar.

Mid-October 1941: The deportation of Jews to extermination camps begins.

January 20, 1942: The Nazis hold the Wannsee Conference to discuss the "Final Solution to the Jewish problem."

April 19, 1943: The Warsaw Ghetto Uprising begins.

August 2, 1943: Prisoners at the Treblinka death camp rise up in revolt. Some escape, but most are killed.

October 14, 1943: Prisoners at the Sobibór death camp rebel. Some escape, but most are killed.

October 7, 1944: Prisoners at Auschwitz-Birkenau blow up one of the crematoria and attempt escape. Again, most are killed.

1944–1945: As Allied forces close in, the Nazis attempt to empty concentration camps, forcing inmates on death marches.

January 27, 1945: The Soviets liberate Auschwitz.

April 30, 1945: Hitler commits suicide in the Führerbunker in Berlin.

May 5, 1945: US troops liberate the Mauthausen camp, the last remaining concentration camp.

May 8, 1945: The Allies accept Germany's unconditional surrender.

November 20, 1945–October 1, 1946: Nazi war criminals are tried at Nuremberg. Several are sentenced to death.

May 14, 1948: Israel becomes a Jewish state. Many Holocaust survivors move there.

GLOSSARY

abdicate To renounce one's throne.

anti-Semitic Prejudiced against the Jews.

armistice An agreement between two warring countries to make peace. Also called a cease-fire or a truce.

Aryan A person of Germanic or Nordic ancestry, characterized by having blond hair and blue eyes. The Nazis believed Aryans comprised a master race.

autocratic Describing a person who does not concern himself or herself with the opinions or desires of others.

concentration camp Camps that concentrated prisoners in one place. Initially, the Nazis used concentration camps to detain political opponents, such as Communists, without trial. In time, all manner of "undesirables" were imprisoned in these camps, including Jews. Concentration camps were not intended to be killing centers per se. The purpose of these camps was to terrorize anyone who refused to conform. Still, due to harsh camp conditions, many prisoners died in concentration camps.

coup An illegal seizure of governmental power.

crematorium (plural crematoria) A facility for burning bodies.

denazification The attempt to rid German society, culture, and government of all vestiges of Nazism.

extermination camps Camps designed for the express purpose of murdering all who entered them, usually as soon as they arrived. Also called death camps.

genocide The deliberate killing of large numbers of members of a particular national, ethnic, racial, or religious group.

ghetto An area within a city that contains a specific segregated group. During World War II, Jewish ghettos were effectively urban prisons.

Holocaust The systematic murder of some six million Jews by Nazi Germany. Among Jews, the Holocaust is also known as the Shoah, which is Hebrew for "destruction."

indoctrinate To teach a group a set of beliefs or ideals without considering other positions.

inflation Describes an increase in prices and/or a decrease in the purchasing power of a particular currency.

partisan A member of an armed organization that fights an occupying force.

pogrom An organized attempt to slaughter helpless members of an ethnic or religious group, particularly the Jews in Russia and eastern Europe.

propaganda Biased or misleading information distributed to promote a particular political point of view or cause.

reparations Moneys paid to make amends for wrongdoing. The Germans were forced to pay reparations to the Allies after World War I.

Star of David A Jewish symbol. It features two interlaced triangles, in the shape of a six-pointed star.

treaty A document signed by two or more countries to state their formal agreement on a particular matter.

Zionist One who believes that the Jews should have their own state.

Books

Frank, Anne. *Anne Frank: The Diary of a Young Girl.* Translated by B. M. Mooyaart-Doubleday. New York: Bantam, reissued 1993.

Klempner, Mark. *The Heart Has Reasons: Holocaust Rescuers and Their Stories of Courage.* Cleveland, OH: Pilgrim Press, 2006.

Wiesel, Elie. *Night.* New York: Hill and Wang, 2006.

Websites

Auschwitz-Birkenau Memorial and Museum
http://auschwitz.org/en/
This website offers a glimpse of life at Auschwitz-Birkenau, one of several Nazi death camps.

The United States Holocaust Museum
https://www.ushmm.org
This is the online home of the United States Holocaust Museum, in Washington, DC, with links to dozens of Holocaust articles and photographs.

Yad Vashem
http://www.yadvashem.org
This is the website for the Yad Vashem World Holocaust Remembrance Center, an Israeli museum devoted to safeguarding the memory of the Holocaust and imparting its meaning to future generations.

Videos

Day in Auschwitz

https://www.youtube.com/watch?v=9IezXBcNdJY&feature= youtu.be

Kitty Hart, who entered Auschwitz at the age of seventeen, returns to the camp with two young women to share what happened there.

Francine's Interview in *Human the Movie*

https://www.youtube.com/watch?v=gXGfngjmwLA

In this video, a Holocaust survivor named Francine Christophe tells a very moving story about life at the Bergen-Belsen concentration camp.

60 Minutes: Sir Nicholas Winton "Saving the Children"

https://www.youtube.com/watch?v=c0aoifNziKQ

This video tells the story of a British man named Nicholas Winton who found safe passage from Czechoslovakia to Britain for some 669 children and homes for them all.

Films

Defiance (2008). This movie, starring Daniel Craig and Liev Schreiber, recounts the story of the Bielski partisans.

The Pianist (2002). Adrien Brody plays Jewish musician Władysław Szpilman, imprisoned in the Warsaw ghetto.

Schindler's List (1993). This Oscar-winning movie recounts the tale of Oskar Schindler, who saved some 1,200 Jewish workers during the Holocaust.

SELECTED BIBLIOGRAPHY

Books

Aronsfeld, Caesar C. *The Text of the Holocaust: A Study of the Nazi Extermination Propaganda, 1919-1945.* Marblehead, MA: Micah Publications, 1985.

Bankier, David. "The Use of Antisemitism in Nazi Wartime Propaganda." In *The Holocaust and History: The Known, the Unknown, the Disputed, and the Reexamined,* edited by Michael Berenbaum, pp. 44. Bloomington, IN: Indiana University Press, 2002.

Berenbaum, Michael. *The World Must Know: The History of the Holocaust as Told in the United States Holocaust Memorial Museum.* Baltimore, MD: Johns Hopkins University Press, 2005.

Dederichs, Mario R. *Heydrich: The Face of Evil.* Havertown, PA: Casemate, 2009.

Eisenhower, General Dwight D. *Letters to Mamie.* Edited by John S. D. Eisenhower. New York: Doubleday, 1978.

Elon, Amos. *The Pity of It All: A History of the Jews in Germany, 1743-1933.* New York: Macmillan, 2002.

Fleming, Gerald. *Hitler and the Final Solution.* Berkeley, CA: University of California Press, 1987.

Fortna, Virginia Page. *Peace Time: Cease-Fire Agreements and the Durability of Peace.* Princeton NJ: Princeton University Press, 2004.

Fritz, Stephen G. *Ostkrieg: Hitler's War of Extermination in the East.* Lexington, KY: University Press of Kentucky, 2011.

Gilbert, Martin. *The Holocaust: The Jewish Tragedy.* New York: Collins, 1986.

Gordon, Sarah Ann. *Hitler, Germans, and the Jewish Question.* Princeton, NJ: Princeton University Press, 1984.

Johnson, Paul. *A History of the Jews.* New York: Harper Perennial, 1988.

Lifton, Robert Jay. *The Nazi Doctors: Medical Killing and the Psychology of Genocide.* New York: Basic Books, 1986.

Luther, Martin. *On the Jews and Their Lies.* Los Angeles, CA: Christian Nationalist Crusade, 1948.

Manchester, William, and Paul Reid. *The Last Lion: Winston Spencer Churchill: Defender of the Realm, 1940–1965.* New York: Little Brown, 2012.

Phayer, Michael. *The Catholic Church and the Holocaust, 1930-1965.* Bloomington, IN: Indiana University Press, 2000.

Polonsky, A. *The Jews in Poland and Russia, Volume III, 1914 to 2008.* Oxford, UK: Littman Library of Jewish Civilization, 2012.

Schleunes, Karl A. *The Twisted Road to Auschwitz: Nazi Policy Toward German Jews, 1933–1939.* Champaign, IL: University of Illinois Press, 1990.

Shirer, William L. *The Rise and Fall of the Third Reich: A History of Nazi Germany.* New York: Simon & Schuster, 2011.

Smith, David Livingstone. *Less Than Human: Why We Demean, Enslave, and Exterminate Others.* New York: Macmillan, 2011.

Tec, Nechama. *Defiance.* Oxford, UK: Oxford University Press, 2008.

Online Articles

Agence France Press. "Last Warsaw Ghetto Revolt Commander Honours Fallen Comrades." *European Jewish* Press, April 20, 2007.

"Anti-Jewish Laws." Alpha History. Accessed May 16, 2016. http://alphahistory.com/holocaust/anti-jewish-laws/#sthash. qY85mBs5.dpuf.

"The Bielski Brothers." Holocaust Education & Archive Research Team. Accessed May 16, 2016. http://www.holocaustresearchproject. org/revolt/bielski.html.

"Blood Libel: A False and Incendiary Claim Against Jews." Anti-Defamation League. Accessed May 2, 2016. http://www.adl. org/anti-semitism/united-states/c/what-is-the-blood-libel.html.

"Convention on the Prevention and Punishment of the Crime of Genocide." United Nations Treaty Collection, January 12, 1951. https://treaties.un.org/doc/Publication/UNTS/Volume%2078/ volume-78-I-1021-English.pdf.

Dimbleby, Richard. "Liberation of Belsen." BBC News, April 15, 2005. http://news.bbc.co.uk/2/hi/in_depth/4445811.stm.

"Evian Conference." This Month in Holocaust History. Accessed May 16, 2016. http://www.yadvashem.org/yv/en/exhibitions/ this_month/resources/evian_conference.asp.

"Evian Conference." Jewish Virtual Library. Accessed May 16, 2016. http://www.jewishvirtuallibrary.org/jsource/judaica/ ejud_0002_0006_0_06165.html.

Hall, Alan. "Revealed: How the Nazis Helped German Companies Bosch, Mercedes, Deutsche Bank and VW Get VERY Rich Using 300,000 Concentration Camp Slaves." *Daily Mail*, June 20,

2014. http://www.dailymail.co.uk/news/article-2663635/ Revealed-How-Nazis-helped-German-companies-Bosch-Mercedes-Deutsche-Bank-VW-VERY-rich-using-slave-labor.html.

"Hitler's Inner Circle: The 10 Most Powerful Men in Nazi Germany." War History Online. May 29, 2015. http://www. warhistoryonline.com/war-articles/hitlers-inner-circle-the-10-most-powerful-men-in-nazi-germany.html.

"The Holocaust: A Learning Site for Students." United States Holocaust Memorial Museum. Accessed May 16, 2016. https://www. ushmm.org/learn/students/the-holocaust-a-learning-site-for-students.

"Holocaust Memorial Center." Holocaust Memorial Center: Zekelman Family Campus. Accessed May 16, 2016. http://www. holocaustcenter.org/home.

"Jewish Population of Europe in 1933: Population Data by Country." United States Holocaust Memorial Museum, Accessed May 16, 2016. https://www.ushmm.org/wlc/en/article. php?ModuleId=10005161.

Kimel, Alexander. "Holocaust Resistance." Humanities and Social Sciences Online. December 2, 1998. http://h-net.msu.edu/cgi-bin/logbrowse.pl?trx=vx&list=h-holocaust&month=9812&week=a &msg=L9lVtqlk3cxYYQe3K8HC1w&user=&pw=.

"Kristallnacht." United States Holocaust Memorial Museum. Accessed May 16, 2016. https://www.ushmm.org/wlc/en/article. php?ModuleId=10005201.

"Liberation." United States Holocaust Memorial Museum. Accessed May 15, 2016. https://www.ushmm.org/outreach/en/article. php?ModuleId=10007724.

"Mein Kampf." Encyclopedia Britannica Online. Accessed May 16, 2016. http://www.britannica.com/topic/Mein-Kampf.

"Nazi Propaganda and Censorship." United States Holocaust Memorial Museum. Accessed May 16, 2016. https://www.ushmm.org/outreach/en/article.php?ModuleId=10007678.

"The Nuremberg Trials." United States Holocaust Memorial Museum. Accessed May 15, 2016. https://www.ushmm.org/outreach/en/article.php?ModuleId=10007722.

Rees, Laurence. "Hitler's Invasion of Russia in World War Two." BBC History, March 30, 2011. http://www.bbc.co.uk/history/worldwars/wwtwo/hitler_russia_invasion_01.shtml.

"The Road to War: Germany: 1919-1939." The Authentic History Center. Accessed May 16, 2016. http://www.authentichistory.com/1930-1939/4-roadtowar/1-germany.

"Russian Revolution." History.com, January 1, 2009. http://www.history.com/topics/russian-revolution.

Stevenson, David. "Aftermath of the First World War." The British Library. Accessed May 16, 2016. http://www.bl.uk/world-war-one/articles/aftermath.

"The United States, the Soviet Union, and the End of World War II." US Department of State Archive. Accessed May 16, 2016. http://2001-2009.state.gov/r/pa/ho/pubs/fs/46345.htm.

"Wilson's Fourteen Points, 1918. " Department of State, Office of the Historian. Accessed May 12, 2016. https://history.state.gov/milestones/1914-1920/fourteen-points.

INDEX

Page numbers in **boldface** are illustrations. Entries in **boldface** are glossary terms.

Kate Shoup has written more than thirty-five books and has edited hundreds more. For Cavendish Square, Kate has written about athletes, celebrities, history, culture, science, and dangerous drugs. When not working, Kate loves to ski, read, ride her motorcycle, and watch IndyCar races. She lives in Indianapolis with her husband, her daughter, and their dog.